Five-Minute Activities for Business English

Cambridge Handbooks for Language Teachers

This is a series of practical guides for teachers of English and other languages. Illustrative examples are usually drawn from the field of English as a foreign or second language, but the ideas and techniques described can equally well be used in the teaching of any language.

Recent titles in this series:

Five-Minute Activities for Business English

Paul Emmerson and Nick Hamilton

CAMBRIDGE
UNIVERSITY PRESS

CAMBRIDGE UNIVERSITY PRESS
Cambridge, New York, Melbourne, Madrid, Cape Town, Singapore, São Paulo

CAMBRIDGE UNIVERSITY PRESS
The Edinburgh Building, Cambridge CB2 2RU, UK

www.cambridge.org
Information on this title: www.cambridge.org/9780521547413

First published 2005

Printed in the United Kingdom at the University Press, Cambridge

Typeface: Adobe Sabon 10/13 pt   *System:* QuarkXPress™   [SE]

A catalogue record for this book is available from the British Library

ISBN-13 978-0-521-54741-3 paperback
ISBN-10 0-521-54741-5 paperback

Contents

> **See also** *Mini-presentations 55 / 'Wh' questions 68 /
> Things in common 68 / Time management 69 / Current
> project 71 / Fact or fiction? 72 / I'll never forget 72 /
> Brainstorming collocations 90 / Devowelled words 92 /
> Lexical dominoes 92 / Hot seat 94 / Dictionary search 95 /
> If it was up to me . . . 104*

> **See also** *IT and me 30 / E-commerce 31 / Mini-
> presentations 55 / 'Wh' questions 68 / Things in
> common 68 / Brainstorming collocations 90 / Devowelled
> words 92 / Lexical dominoes 92 / Hot seat 94 / Dictionary
> search 95 / Expanding sentences 100 / In my office 103*

Contents

Contents

> See also *SWOT analysis* 12 / *Budgets* 27 / *Effective
> performance* 61 / *First few minutes* 62 / *Follow-up email*
> 74 / *Hot seat* 94 / *Correct yourself* 104 / *Revise key phrases*
> 105 / *Role play changes* 109

10   Business communication skills: presentations

> See also *My job and me* 6 / *What's your background?* 9 /
> *Describing your company* 11 / *Organigrams* 11 /
> *The clarification game* 48 / *Phonological chunking* 87 /
> *Hot seat* 94 / *Correct yourself* 104 / *Revise key phrases* 105

11   Business communication skills: social English

> See also *What's your job?* 5 / *Perks and drags* 5 / *What's
> your background?* 9 / *Effective performance* 61 / *'Wh'
> questions* 68 / *Things in common* 68 / *I'll never forget* 72 /
> *Follow-up email* 74 / *Passing notes* 78 / *Hot seat* 94 /
> *Correct yourself* 104 / *Revise key phrases* 105 / *Role play
> changes* 109

12 Language work: speaking

> **See also** Most activities for *Business topics* and *Business communication skills* / *Response to a text* 84 / *Hot seat* 94 / *Correct yourself* 104 / *Role play changes* 109

13 Language work: writing

> **See also** *Career plans* 10 / *Describing your company* 11 / *Company plans* 14 / *Product profiles* 15 / *An entrepreneur I admire* 22 / *Spending, wasting, saving* 26 / *Opening the meeting* 46 / *'Wh' questions* 68 / *Putting back the grammar* 99 / *Expanding sentences* 100 / *Five-minute dictogloss* 101 / *In my office* 103 / *If it was up to me . . .* 104 / *Correct yourself* 104

14 Language work: listening

> **See also** Activities for *telephoning* / *It's a good story, isn't it?* 67 / *Response to a text* 84 / *Questioning the text* 85 / *Figures in the news* 86 / *Phonological chunking* 87 / *Five-minute dictogloss* 101

> **See also** *Tracking shares* 29 / *Internet news* 31 / *Researching your own culture* 34 / *Follow-up email* 74 / *Incorrect summaries* 82 / *What does that stand for?* 94 / *Business metaphors* 98 / *Putting back the grammar* 99

> **See also** *Saying figures* 23 / *To read or not to read, that is the question* 59 / *Dictating news headlines* 80 / *Listen and count* 83

See also *Job skills 4 / Business documents 16 / Describing trends 23 / Pelmanism 25 / Financial statements 27 / Internet translation tools 32 / The clarification game 48 / Disagreeing 49 / Problems, problems 51 / Signposts 57 / Standard exchanges 64 / What do you say when . . . ? 65 / Menus 66 / Listen and count 83 / More than single words 85 / Stress patterns 88 / DIY gapfill 106 / Cover it up (two columns) 107 / Cover it up (gapfill) 108 / Noticing language in a tapescript 109*

18 Language work: grammar

See also *What's your job?* 5 / *Dream job* 6 / *Career plans* 10 / *Company plans* 14 / *Describing trends* 23 / *Diplomatic language* 50 / *Follow-up questions* 63 / '*Wh*' *questions* 68 / *DIY gapfill* 106

19 Exploiting coursebooks

See also Activities for *listening* and *reading* / *Standard exchanges* 64 / *Reformulate a letter to an email* 76 / *The purpose of this report* 79 / *Phonological chunking* 87 / *Categorising vocabulary* 96 / *Putting back the grammar* 99 / *English → L1 → English* 102

Thanks and Acknowledgements

The authors would like to thank Penny Ur for her valuable contributions to the book, Lyn Strutt for her thorough copy-editing, and Frances Amrani for co-ordinating everything so efficiently.

The authors and publishers are grateful to the following for permission to reproduce copyright material. It has not been possible to identify the sources of all the material used and in such cases the publishers would welcome information from copyright owners.
p.37 'Flight to Rubovia' adapted from an activity in *The Cross-cultural Business Pocketbook* by kind permission of John Mattock Management Pocketbooks 1999; p.79 Extract from *Business Reports in English* by Jeremy Comfort, Rod Revell and Chris Stott, CUP 1984; p.81 Extracts from *Working in English* by Leo Jones, CUP 2001; Extract from *Getting Ahead* by Sarah Jones-Macziola and Greg White, CUP 1993; pp.87 and 99 Extracts from *English 365* by Bob Dignen, Steve Flanders and Simon Sweeney, CUP 2004; p.99 Extract from *New International Business English* by Leo Jones and Richard Alexander, CUP 1996; p.107 Extract from *Business Vocabulary in Use* by Bill Mascull, CUP 2002.

The publisher has used its best endeavours to ensure that the URLs for external websites referred to in this book are correct and active at the time of going to press. However, the publisher has no responsibility for the websites and can make no guarantee that a site will remain live or that the content is or will remain appropriate.

Introduction

The need for short activities in Business English

There are many situations where Business English teachers need short activities, for example:

- a warmer to provide the transition from the students' daily life to the world of the Business English classroom
- a lead-in for whatever business topic or communication skill will be the main focus of the lesson
- an activity to introduce or extend a speaking or writing task
- an idea for working with an interesting reading or listening text
- an activity to focus on or review an area of vocabulary, grammar or pronunciation
- an activity to practise something covered in a previous lesson
- a way to round off the lesson

As well as being useful in putting lessons together, short activities may also help in dealing with the unpredictable situations common to Business English teaching such as erratic attendance on in-company courses, covering for another teacher at short notice, or doing tutorials with individual students to cater for specific needs.

The activities

Organisation
We have organised the activities under the following headings and sub-headings to make it easy for you to find something appropriate for the lesson you are planning:

Business topics: jobs and careers, the company, products and services, management and marketing, money and finance, IT, cultural awareness. These activities lead into the main focus of a lesson, in terms of both business content and key language.

Business communication skills: telephoning, meetings and negotiations, presentations, social English. These activities cover the main business communication skills, looking at the nature of the skill itself and the relevant language.

Language work: speaking; writing; listening; reading; pronunciation; vocabulary; grammar; exploiting coursebooks. These are activities for the four language skills and general activities to review and extend language that the students have recently learnt. Many of these activities will be familiar to General English teachers.

Level
The activities will work over a range of levels. We have indicated the recommended level for each activity, but many of the activities can be adapted to other levels.

Preparation
We have tried to keep this to a minimum, and in most cases all you need is a whiteboard or flipchart to write on. Many activities have a short amount of text to prepare on the board beforehand, and we imagine that you will do this before the lesson or while students are working heads-down on another activity. For some activities we have given references to websites and students need to be in front of a computer. We have also included a few ready-made activities that can be enlarged and photocopied.

Timing
Although the activities are all designed to be completed within five minutes, many of them can be extended, some even allowing for whole lessons to be built around them. We have indicated this in the optional Follow-up sections.

Business Content
We have aimed to cover the main areas of international business in a realistic way that will be familiar to business students, without going into language that is too technical. The activities will therefore work with both pre-experience and post-experience learners. As with most Business English materials, this book assumes that the teacher has a basic knowledge of the business world but not necessarily any direct experience of working in business.

We see the teaching of Business English as a process of working creatively with the business content supplied by the students that we as teachers of English then shape in terms of its language. We hope the activities in this book will give you some ideas for working with this process and that you enjoy using them.

Paul Emmerson and Nick Hamilton, May 2004

Needs analysis

Focus Conducting a needs analysis
Level Intermediate – Advanced
Preparation Write up on the board a list of possible business topics and communication skills that you could cover on the course. See Box 1 for an example. Alternatively, photocopy and distribute Box 1.
Note Suitable for Day One, Lesson One

Box 1   List of topics and skills

Business Topics

Management
Sales and Marketing
Finance and Accounting
Production and Operations
Human Resources
Cultural Awareness
Recent Business News

Communication Skills

Presentations
Meetings and Discussions
Negotiating
Telephoning
Social English
Writing emails
Writing reports

© CAMBRIDGE UNIVERSITY PRESS 2005

Procedure

1 Refer to the boardwork. Hand out board pens round the group. Ask students to come up to the board two or three at a time and write:
   ✓✓   for things that are very important for them
   ✓   for things that are quite important for them
   (nothing) for things that are not important for them
2 Note down the priorities, and tell them you will take these into account when planning the course.

Follow-up
• Discuss with the group their priorities and the reasons for them.
• Invite them to add more items to the list if they want, and say how many ticks they would give them.

Business topics: jobs and careers

1.1 Job skills

Focus	Introducing vocabulary for skills and abilities
Level	Elementary – Advanced

Procedure

1   Write on the board one job name, e.g. *sales manager, accountant, IT systems manager, Chief Executive Officer, journalist*, or choose one that several members of the group have or know about.
2   Brainstorm and write on the board the skills and abilities that you need to do this job. Some typical ideas for a variety of jobs are given in Box 2, but follow whatever the students suggest.

Box 2   Examples of skills and abilities

being good with figures/people/technical issues
being a good administrator
being good at organising your time
having a good understanding of the market
liking challenges
working well in a team
being a good communicator

Follow-up
- Choose another job to generate more ideas.
- Students write down the skills and abilities they need to do their own job. Afterwards the teacher can collect them in and then read them out in random order. Other students have to guess whose job is being described.

1.2 What's your job?

Focus	Asking about aspects of jobs
Level	Elementary – Intermediate

Procedure

1 Elicit and write on the board a few questions to ask people about their jobs. For example:

Can you work from home?
Do you have to work long hours?
Does your work involve a lot of travelling?

2 Invent a new job for yourself. Tell students that you have changed your job and they have to guess what you do now. They should do this by asking you questions, but you will only answer with *yes* or *no*.

3 If there is time, the student who guesses your job then thinks of one and is questioned by the other students.

Follow-up
Continue for a short while, then summarise the questions the students used on the board.

1.3 Perks and drags

Focus	Discussing job descriptions
Level	Elementary – Advanced

Procedure

1 Write on the board:

One of the perks of the job is . . . (+ -ing)
(+ -ing) . . . is a bit of a drag

2 Check the students understand the vocabulary. A *perk* is an extra benefit that you get from your job, in addition to your pay. Typical perks are a company car, or a laptop computer, or language lessons. A *drag* is something that is boring or unexciting and that you don't like doing. Typical drags are writing reports, having to make a long car journey to work every morning, or attending unnecessary meetings. The word *drag* is used mostly in informal speech.

3 Use the sentence beginning and ending on the board to give a few examples from your teaching job.

5

4   Students complete the sentences for themselves, then compare with a partner.

Follow-up
You can explore in a class discussion the different sorts of incentive that people get (beyond their salary), and also what to do about aspects of their work that they don't enjoy.

1.4 My job and me

Focus	Discussing job responsibilities
Level	Elementary – Advanced

Procedure

1   Say to the students:

> *'When you start a job, you do more or less what your boss expects, more or less what the previous person did, more or less what the job description says. But then after some time . . . you bring something new to the job, you change how things are done, you make a difference because of who you are.'*

2   Ask students to think of one way that they have 'made a difference' in their current job, i.e. how they have developed the job through their own initiative.

3   Students tell the group (as many reports as you have time for).

1.5 Dream job

Focus	Describing your perfect occupation
Level	Elementary – Advanced

Procedure

1   Write on the board:

<u>Dream job</u>
If I wasn't a . . ., I'd like to be a . . . .

2   Complete the sentence for yourself, and write it on the board underneath. For example:

If I wasn't a teacher, I'd like to be a potter.

3   Respond briefly to any questions that your statement provokes.
4   Ask the students to write down their dream job, and provide vocabulary of occupations as needed. They share their ideas in small groups and answer questions.

Follow-up
Ask students for examples of people they know who have radically changed their career. Why did they do it? Was it successful? How easy was it to do?

1.6 What would your boss say?

| Focus | Talking about your own job in the role of someone else |
| Level | Intermediate – Advanced |

Procedure
1   Ask for a volunteer who is going to take on the identity of their own boss. This person will come to the front of the class and answer questions about themselves in real life, but speaking in the role of their boss.
2   The other students question the 'boss' (the volunteer in role) about the 'employee' (the volunteer in real life). For example: What are his/her strong/weak points? What do you think he/she will be doing two years from now?

Follow-up
• Do the same activity, but the volunteer takes on the identity of one of their own subordinates. They will now answer questions about their 'boss' (the volunteer in real life).
• This activity could introduce a lesson on Human Resources.

1.7 Interview experience

| Focus | Discussing job interviews |
| Level | Elementary – Advanced |

Procedure
1   Tell the students about an interview that you had.
2   Invite them to tell the group about their own experience of job interviews: what is the best or worst one they have ever had?

Follow-up
- You might discuss the different ways in which an interview can be conducted (formal, with a panel of people on the other side of the table; informal, with a chat over a cup of coffee).
- You might discuss whether students have come across any unusual techniques, e.g. psychological tests, using graphology to analyse handwriting.
- You might discuss interviewing and selection procedures in their own company: How is it done? Who decides? Do they have any suggestions for changes?

1.8 Interview questions

Focus Discussing job interviews
Level Intermediate – Advanced

Procedure

1 Ask students what questions interviewers in their company ask a candidate for a job (or which ones they are often asked in job interviews). Elicit some examples and write them on the board. See Box 3 for typical interview questions.

Box 3   Some typical interview questions

Tell me something about yourself.
What have you learnt in your current job?
Why do you want to leave your current job?
What are your strong points?
What are your weak points?
What are your career objectives?

---

2 Discuss in the class: Which are the questions that show the most about a candidate?

Follow-up
- Other questions to discuss might include which ones are the most difficult to answer.
- In pairs or groups, students choose three of the questions on the board and discuss how they personally would answer them.

1.9 Career stages

Focus Discussing significant events and changes in your career
Level Elementary – Advanced

Procedure

1 Write up on the board four dates, places, or names that have been significant in your career. Start talking about them and encourage students to ask you questions.
2 Students then write down their own four dates, places, or names. They get together in pairs or small groups and explain them to each other. Encourage them to ask each other questions.

Follow-up
One student repeats for the whole class, writing the four items on the board and telling the class about them. Other students ask questions.

1.10 What's your background?

Focus Summarising your life and career
Level Elementary – Advanced

Procedure

1 Write up on the board:

What's your background?

Make sure the students know the meaning of *background* in this context (the type of education, work and experience you have had in your life).
2 Tell the students that this question is very common when people meet for the first time in a business situation. To answer it, you need to summarise your whole life in about 30 seconds!
3 Give the students an example of how to answer using your own life and career (or possibly read out a previous student's answer). It's best to make it up spontaneously as you go. In Box 4 there is an example for one of the authors of this book that takes about 30 seconds to say at normal speaking speed.
4 Tell the students that you want them to do the same. They work in pairs, each telling the other their background as you did in the demonstration.

9

Box 4   Example for 'What's your background?'

I was born and brought up in London, then I went to university in the north of England. I lived in Manchester for many years, working as a teacher in community education. In my mid thirties I moved to Portugal, and I lived in Lisbon, working as a freelance Business English trainer. I did that for six years. I came back to the UK in 1996, and I've had two parallel jobs since then. Over the summer I teach at International House, London, but most of the year I write books in the field of Business English. I also do a bit of teacher training.

Follow-up

To consolidate the activity, the students can work on their background speech for homework. Then in the next class they perform their speech publicly, and they have to say it without notes.

1.11 Career plans

Focus	Writing about possible developments in your career
Level	Elementary – Advanced
Preparation	Write on the board, or photocopy and distribute, the text in Box 5.

Box 5   Career plans

Over the next few years
     I intend to . . .
     And I'm going to try to . . .
     If possible, I'd also like to . . .
     And I hope to . . . , although I know it won't be easy.

© CAMBRIDGE UNIVERSITY PRESS 2005

Procedure

1   Establish a clear business/professional context: students are writing about how they can develop their careers, not about their personal lives.
2   Ask students to write 1–2 sentences to complete each sentence beginning.

Follow-up

Students read out their sentences, explaining in more detail and answering questions.

2 Business topics: the company

2.1 Describing your company

Focus	Writing a one-paragraph presentation of your company
Level	Intermediate – Advanced

Procedure

1 Write on the board:

   main products/services   markets   competitors   head office   employees

2 Ask students to write a paragraph describing their company. They have to use all the words on the board, but they can use them in any order.

2.2 Organigrams

Focus	Discussing company structure
Level	Elementary – Advanced
Note	Only suitable if students work for different companies

Procedure

1 Ask students to draw a rough organigram of their company on a piece of paper. See the example in Box 6 below.

Box 6   Example of an organigram

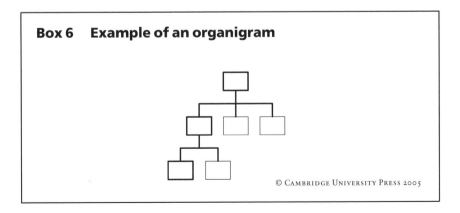

---

2 Students get together in pairs or groups and explain their diagrams. Encourage them to ask each other questions: How is the work divided between different people? What exactly is their own responsibility?

2.3 Logos

Focus Discussing company image
Level Elementary – Advanced

Procedure

1 Draw 2–3 well-known logos on the board. For example the London Underground logo:
Other logos that are easy to draw include McDonald's 'golden arches', the Nike 'swoosh' and the Shell 'seashell'.
2 For each logo, ask the students: Why is it effective? What does it represent? What image does it give of the organisation?

Follow-up
Ask a few volunteers to draw their company logo on the board and explain it.

2.4 SWOT analysis

Focus Identifying strong and weak points of your company
Level Intermediate – Advanced
Preparation Draw on the board the diagram in Box 7.
Note SWOT stands for strengths, weaknesses, opportunities, threats

Procedure

1 Check the students understand the vocabulary (*strengths* = strong points; *weaknesses* = weak points; *opportunities* = future chances; *threats* = future dangers). Explain to students that a *SWOT analysis* is a common way in business to get a very quick 'snapshot' of a company and its market.
2 Ask the students to think of one item for each box for their own company. Then, as they are ready, they come to the board and write up their idea. Make sure you have several board markers available so that several students can write at the same time. You will finish with a list of items in each box. (If some students haven't written anything for *weaknesses*, then don't force them to – they may feel it is disloyal.)

Box 7 Diagram for a SWOT analysis

	+	−
Company	Strengths	Weaknesses
Market	Opportunities	Threats

Note: Some items to feed in if the students can't get started are given in Box 8.

Box 8 Typical items in a SWOT analysis

Strengths – good market share, experience of top management, efficient manufacturing process, good brand image, good distribution channels
Weaknesses – small market share, high levels of debt, lack of modern technology, poor distribution channels
Opportunities – possible new markets, growing economy, developments in technology
Threats – slowdown in the economy, success of existing competitors, new competitors, changing consumer tastes

Follow-up
Students discuss and compare their ideas.

Variation
Students can do a personal SWOT analysis for learning English:
– What are your strengths in English?
– What are your weaknesses in English?
– What are your opportunities for practising English?
– What stops you getting better (e.g. using L1 in class too much)?

2.5 Company plans

Focus Writing about possible developments for the company
Level Elementary – Advanced
Preparation Write on the board, or photocopy and distribute, the text in Box 9.

Box 9   Company plans

Next year, one of the major developments in my company is likely to be . . .
And I think we'll probably . . .
Also, we might . . .
But we probably won't . . .

© CAMBRIDGE UNIVERSITY PRESS 2005

Procedure

1   Establish a clear context for each student. For example, some might prefer to write about their department or their functional area (sales, marketing, production) rather than the company as a whole.
2   Ask students to write 1–2 sentences to complete each sentence beginning.

Follow-up

•   Students read out their sentences, explaining in more detail and answering questions.
•   Students can use their ideas (including any clarifications and further ideas from the follow-up discussion) to write a short report.

Business topics: products and services

3.1 Product profiles

Focus	Describing products
Level	Elementary – Advanced
Preparation	Write on the board, or photocopy and distribute, the text in Box 10.

Box 10   Product profiles

It's made in . . . (*country of origin*) . . .
It's sold . . . (*distribution channel*) . . .
It's advertised . . . (*media*) . . .
It's in the . . . (*€40 to €50*) price range.
I bought it because . . . (*your own reason*) . . .

© Cambridge University Press 2005

Procedure

1 Ask the students to pick a personal possession they have with them which they can describe, e.g. a mobile phone, a laptop, a watch, a jacket, a bag. The object needs to be in view, but the students should **keep their choice secret.**

2 Tell them to write a brief description of the object, using the sentence beginnings on the board. They should be careful not to include information that makes it too easy to identify the object.

3 Collect in the pieces of paper. Read out one or two at random and ask the class to guess which (and whose) object is being described.

Follow-up

Ask students to write a fuller description of their object, using their dictionaries to help them. They should focus on the vocabulary needed for size, shape, materials, design, function, features, etc.

Variation
After collecting in the pieces of paper, give them back out again in random order so that everyone gets a new description. Students then read out the descriptions and the class has to guess which (and whose) object is being described.

3.2 USP

Focus	Discussing the main feature of a product or service
Level	Elementary – Advanced

Procedure

1   Write up on the board the letters *USP* and elicit or give what they stand for: *Unique Selling Point* (also *Unique Selling Proposition*).
2   Check the students understand this phrase: a USP is some feature of a product or service that no other competitor product has; it is therefore one of the main reasons that a customer would buy or use it.
3   Ask students to write down the name of their main product or service and one of its USPs.
4   A few students explain their USPs.

Follow-up
•   The students answer questions from the group.
•   Other students explain their USPs in later lessons.

3.3 Business documents

Focus	Defining typical customer-supplier documents
Level	Intermediate – Advanced
Preparation	Write on the board, or photocopy and distribute, the text in Box 11.

Box 11   Customer–supplier documents

inquiry	quotation
invoice	reminder
order	receipt
payment	shipping confirmation

© CAMBRIDGE UNIVERSITY PRESS 2005

Procedure

1 Check that the students understand all the items. Then ask them who would send each one: the customer or the supplier.
Answers:
sent by customer – inquiry, order, payment
sent by supplier – invoice, quotation, reminder, receipt, shipping confirmation
(Note: Students often get confused between *invoice* and *receipt*. An invoice asks for payment; a receipt proves payment has been made.)
2 Ask students to put the documents into a typical sequence.
Answers:
inquiry, quotation, order, shipping confirmation, invoice, reminder, payment, receipt

3.4 Complaints

Focus	Practising a customer services dialogue
Level	Intermediate – Advanced

Procedure

1 Ask students to write down the one most common complaint they receive from customers. They should write down the actual words that a customer might use – one sentence is enough.
2 Divide the class into pairs. The students exchange sentences. Student A reads out their sentence (i.e. taking the role of a complaining customer). Student B replies, as they would in their job, dealing with the complaint. The conversation continues for a few more turns.
3 They change roles: student B reads out their sentence in the role of the complaining customer, and student A deals with the complaint.

Follow-up
• One pair acts out the dialogues again for the whole class.
• The class discusses general techniques for handling complaints.
• Make a list on the board of the specific complaints that the group wrote down. Then the whole class discusses the best way to deal with each one (both techniques and useful language).

Variations
• Instead of students writing down the actual words that a customer might use, the class simply brainstorms a list of typical complaints which you

17

write on the board. Then they do mini-role plays in pairs based on these ideas. (The resulting role plays will be freer, with students having to provide more of the content as they proceed).

- Instead of students doing the mini-role plays in closed pairs, one pair could perform for the class immediately.
- A combination of the above two activities.

4 Business topics: management and marketing

4.1 Management tips

Focus	Introducing the topic of management
Level	Elementary – Advanced

Procedure

1 Ask students to write down two tips that they would give to a new manager in their company.
2 Invite students to come to the board and write up their tips. (If you divide the board into two sections with a vertical line, then two students can be writing at the same time.)
3 Students explain their ideas to the class.

Follow-up

Number the tips on the board. Tell students that they are now going to vote for the four tips that they like best, but they cannot vote for their own. Students first write their four numbers on a piece of paper, then vote in open class for each suggestion by raising hands. Write the totals on the board by each tip, then discuss with the group why the winning tip(s) won.

4.2 Demotivation

Focus	Discussing the topic of motivation
Level	Elementary – Advanced

Procedure

1 Ask the students to write down three things that are guaranteed to demotivate an employee in their company.
2 Divide the students into pairs or threes. They compare their ideas and decide on the 'best' one.
3 The groups share their ideas with the rest of the class.

Follow-up

This activity could introduce a more conventional discussion on motivation at work.

4.3 Is it ethical?

Focus Discussing company policy and 'green' issues
Level Intermediate – Advanced

Procedure

1   Write on the board:

   This product is ethically produced and traded.

   Ask students to suggest what this might involve and write up their ideas.
   For example:

   It doesn't damage the environment.
   The company doesn't exploit workers.
   The company respects human rights.

2   Ask the students to think of companies and products that are ethical.

Follow-up
Discuss with the group: What can be done to encourage companies to
operate on an ethical basis?

4.4 Brand associations

Focus Exploring brands and brand images
Level Elementary – Advanced

Procedure

1   Write a well-known brand name on the board (e.g. Coca-Cola,
    Microsoft, Gucci, Disneyworld, Toyota) and ask students to brainstorm
    the feelings, ideas and images that they associate with it. Encourage them
    to do this as quickly as they can without much thinking.
2   Explore with students where these associations come from. How much
    are they to do with the company's advertising?
3   Repeat for another, contrasting brand.

Follow-up
The above activity can be used to set up a lesson on marketing or
advertising.

4.5 Magazine pictures

Focus	Discussing advertising images
Level	Elementary – Advanced
Preparation	Bring in a selection of magazine pictures without any text (you can have them already pasted onto A4 paper).
Note	The pictures should be general, non-commercial ones, **not** already used as adverts and **not** clearly featuring a particular product.

Procedure

1   Give each pair of students a picture and ask them to decide on a product it could be used to advertise.

2   Students discuss in pairs how the picture could be used and then hold up their picture and tell the group which product it could advertise.

Follow-up

• Students explain why they chose that product for that image. Then they vote on the best idea.

• Look at some pictures that are already used as adverts. Explore in a class discussion how the picture represents the image of the brand.

4.6 What makes a good sales consultant?

Focus	Discussing sales and selling
Level	Elementary – Advanced
Preparation	Write on the board the text in Box 12.

Box 12   Sales consultant

What makes a good sales consultant in your business?

                              %

personality
good appearance
sales technique
product knowledge

Procedure

1   Ask students to write down a percentage figure for each item, to make 100% in total.
2   Ask students to go to the board and write their own percentage figures in a column with their name at the top (if they suggest other factors then those can be added to the list on the board).
3   Students return to their seats and discuss the figures.

4.7   An entrepreneur I admire

> Focus   Introducing the topic of small businesses/start-ups/management
> Level   Intermediate – Advanced
> Preparation   Write on the board, or photocopy and distribute, the text in Box 13.

Box 13   Entrepreneur

An entrepreneur I admire

.... (*name*) is well known in my country because . . .
He/She started the business by . . . (*+-ing*), and now . . .
What's interesting about him/her is . . .
What I really admire about him/her is . . .

© Cambridge University Press 2005

Procedure

1   Check the students understand *entrepreneur* (someone who starts their own business, especially when this involves risks).
2   Use the sentence beginnings on the board to talk about an entrepreneur who is well known internationally, such as Bill Gates. You can complete the sentences yourself, or ask the students to.
3   Ask students to think of an entrepreneur in their own country that they admire. Get them to write down the name and a few facts.
4   Students share their ideas.

Follow-up
Discuss success in business: Why do some people succeed and some fail? What are the most important qualities for a successful entrepreneur?

5   Business topics: money and finance

5.1   Saying figures

Focus	Pronouncing longer numbers, decimals, fractions
Level	Elementary – Advanced

Procedure

1   Write on the board a series of figures, including longer numbers, decimals and fractions. For example:

1,450	*6½*	*2.6*
186,000	*1¾*	*80m²*

2   Ask students to write down how they would say the numbers. Correct as necessary, and discuss any tricky points. Some likely mistakes are: wrong insertions or omissions of *and*; addition of a plural 's' to *hundred* and *thousand*; saying *sixty-six* instead of *six six* after a decimal point.

Follow-up
Invite students to bring to class next time company documents or website printouts with figures on them. Check with the class how to say these.

Variation
Do the same activity for dates and years.

5.2   Describing trends

Focus	Describing and explaining changes
Level	Intermediate – Advanced
Preparation	Prepare the boardwork in Box 14, with *because* written more boldly or in a different colour. Include the sketch graph as part of the boardwork. Alternatively, photocopy and distribute Box 14.

Procedure

1   Ask the students to choose **one** of the topics in the list on the left-hand side of the board, and then draw a very simple graph to show its

fluctuations. Refer to the graph on the board as an example. Numbers on the vertical axis are **not** needed, but the horizontal axis should show the timescale (months/quarters/years). One minute should be enough to sketch the graph.

2 Divide the class into pairs. Tell the students that they should use their graph to describe and explain the movements up and down to their partner. They should try to use expressions from the board.

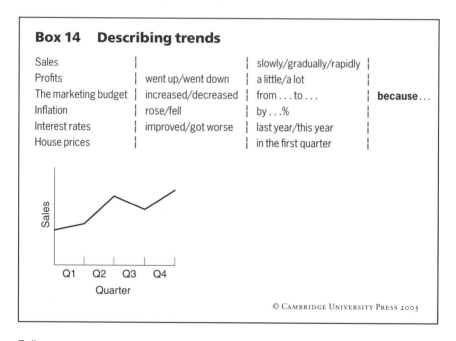

Box 14 Describing trends

Sales		slowly/gradually/rapidly	
Profits	went up/went down	a little/a lot	
The marketing budget	increased/decreased	from . . . to . . .	**because** . . .
Inflation	rose/fell	by . . .%	
Interest rates	improved/got worse	last year/this year	
House prices		in the first quarter	

Sales / Quarter graph: Q1 Q2 Q3 Q4

© Cambridge University Press 2005

Follow-up

Regroup the students into new pairs. They repeat the exercise, but this time their partner should ask questions to force them to explain in more detail (and there is no time limit). You might want to elicit some phrases to the board first:

Can you explain that in a little more detail?
What were the reasons for that?
Can you be a little more specific?
I'm sorry, I don't understand. Can you go over that again?

Variation

Students describe and explain the trend without a graph to help them. They can do this either as the main activity (higher levels), or as a repeat with a new partner after they have first had the graph to help them.

5.3 Pelmanism

Focus	Describing financial trends
Level	Intermediate – Advanced
Preparation	Make a set of cards of synonyms using useful terms from business (an example of one set is shown in Box 15, which you could photocopy onto card and cut up). You will need one set for every four students.
Note	It is important to use card, not paper, as the words must not show through.

Box 15   Matching words for playing Pelmanism

rise	increase
soar	rocket
fall	decrease
slump	plummet
peak	reach a high
bottom out	reach a low
recover	pick up
level off	flatten out
fluctuate	vary
stand at	be at

Procedure

Shuffle the cards so that they are in a random order and lay them face down on a table. Students take it in turns to turn over two cards. If the words are **exact** synonyms (as in the pairs on the same line above), the person who turned them over keeps them. If not, they turn them back, and the next person turns over two cards. The aim of the game is to pick up as many matching pairs as possible.

Follow-up
You might explore the many other synonyms of these words.

5.4 Spending, wasting, saving

Focus	Writing about costs and budgets
Level	Intermediate – Advanced
Preparation	Write on the board, or photocopy and distribute, the text in Box 16.

Box 16   Spending, wasting, saving

Last year in my company we : spent a lot of money on . . .
: wasted a lot of money on . . .
: saved a lot of money by . . . (+ -*ing*)

© CAMBRIDGE UNIVERSITY PRESS 2005

Procedure

1 Establish a clear context for each student. For example, some might prefer to write about their department or their functional area (sales, marketing, production) rather than the company as a whole.
2 Ask students to write 1–2 alternatives to complete each sentence.

Follow-up
• Students read out their sentences, explaining in more detail and answering questions.
• Students use their ideas (including any clarifications and further ideas from the follow-up discussion) to write a short report on budget control in their company.

Variation
Substitute *time* for *money* in Box 16.

5.5 Budgets

Focus Discussing financial plans
Level Intermediate – Advanced

Procedure

1   Write up on the board the word *budget* and elicit or give the meaning: an amount of money you have to spend, or your plan to spend it.
2   Ask students to write down the name of one particular budget that they deal with: it could be the advertising budget for a new product, the budget for a project, the budget for an event, or even an expenses budget for a foreign business trip.
3   One student tells the group the name of their budget, and gives a little background. The others (including the teacher) ask questions. For example: Approximately how big is the budget? How was that figure decided?

Follow-up

*   If their budget was increased by 10% tomorrow, what would the students spend it on?
*   In the case of a budget that is already being spent (i.e. not just a planned budget), students can give one way that the money is being well spent, and one way it is not being so well spent.

5.6 Financial statements

Focus Looking at the profit and loss account and balance sheet
Level Intermediate – Advanced
Preparation Write on the board in random order, or photocopy and distribute, the words in Box 17.

Box 17   Vocabulary for a profit and loss account and a balance sheet

operating profit	current liabilities	costs
turnover/revenue	tax	retained profit
stockholders' equity	dividends	profit after tax
current assets	fixed assets	

© CAMBRIDGE UNIVERSITY PRESS 2005

Procedure

1 Ask the students to sort the words into *profit and loss account* and *balance sheet*.

2 Check the answers, then for the remaining time ask the students to put the items in the profit and loss account into order. See answers in Box 18.

Box 18   Standard layout for a profit and loss account and a balance sheet

Profit & Loss Account
Turnover/Revenue
– Costs
= Operating Profit
– Tax
= Profit after Tax
– Dividends
= Retained Profit

Balance Sheet

| Current assets | Current liabilities |
| Fixed assets | Stockholders' equity |

© CAMBRIDGE UNIVERSITY PRESS 2005

Note: *Stockholders' equity* refers to share capital and retained profit.

5.7 Investment portfolio

Focus Discussing investment strategies
Level Intermediate – Advanced

Procedure

1 Tell students they have just won €5 million in a lottery and have to decide how to invest it. In order to spread the risk they will need at least three ideas, and will need to decide the percentage spread between these.

2 Brainstorm and write on the board some ideas for investments. (Likely suggestions are: domestic equities, international equities, government bonds, corporate bonds, and cash in a bank deposit.) According to the level of financial knowledge of the group, you may want to set some other criteria, such as whether they are investing for growth or income, which international markets, other financial instruments like gold and currencies, etc.

3 Students decide on and write down their ideas.

Follow-up
- Write up all the ideas on the board for comparison.
- The class discusses which is the safest, the riskiest, and the most creative investment.
- You might discuss recent movements on the financial markets and the best strategies for investing wisely.

5.8 Tracking shares

Focus	Following financial markets
Level	Intermediate – Advanced
Note	This is a series of short activities over several lessons.

Procedure
First lesson:

1 Ask students to suggest some well-known companies that would be good to invest in, and write the names up on the board.
2 Put students in pairs and ask each pair to choose one of the companies. Tell them that they are going to have a competition to see which share price performs the best. The period of time can be a week, several weeks or even a whole academic year.
3 Check that students know sources for monitoring the price of shares (e.g. financial press, online). They can also type the company name into search engines like Google to see if there is any news about their company.

Homework:
Students find out news about their company, and monitor its share price.

Future lessons:
The pairs report on their share, giving the movement from the previous check and any news items they found. At the end of the time period, find out whose share has gone up the most!

Follow-up
This activity done over a series of weeks provides an opportunity to explore the various influences on the financial markets, e.g. market conditions, competitors, news.

6   Business topics: information technology

6.1 IT and me

Focus Discussing information technology
Level Intermediate – Advanced
Preparation Write on the board the words *IT and me* and then **one** of the sentence beginnings in Box 19. Alternatively, photocopy and distribute Box 19.

Box 19   Sentence beginnings for discussing IT

IT and me

What I find most exciting about IT at the moment is . . .
The single greatest change in our IT system over the last few years has been . . .
The biggest change in our IT system over the next few years is probably going to be . . .
The biggest disaster we ever had with our IT system was when . . .
If I could upgrade one piece of software tomorrow, it would be . . .
If I could upgrade one piece of hardware tomorrow, it would be . . .
The one thing that would really improve mobile communications in our company is . . .
The company's website is really important because . . .
We could really improve our company website by (+-*ing*) . . .
In order to integrate IT more closely with our other business activities, the best idea would be to . . .

© CAMBRIDGE UNIVERSITY PRESS 2005

Procedure

1   Ask students to write down the sentence beginning on the board (or choose one from the photocopy) and then complete it in their own way.
2   Say that you want a volunteer to tell the group something about the IT system in their company. Ask them to read out their completed sentence, then the rest of the group (and you) can ask questions.

Follow-up

• Invite more volunteers to do the same.
• Repeat for other sentence beginnings on other days.

6.2 What's your favourite website?

Focus	Discussing the Internet
Level	Elementary – Advanced

Procedure

1   Write up on the board:

What's your favourite website?
What's the most useful website you know?

2   Discuss the different ideas with the class.

6.3 E-commerce

Focus	Discussing doing business on the Internet
Level	Elementary – Advanced

Procedure

1   Write up on the board:

How often do you buy things online?
Does your company sell directly to customers online?

2   Discuss the different ideas with the class.

6.4 Internet news

Focus	Reading and summarising a news story from the Internet
Level	Intermediate–Advanced
Preparation	Ensure each student is in front of a computer, looking at one of the sites in Box 20.
Note	Needs one computer per student; particularly suitable for one-to-one

Procedure

1   Ask the students to look at all the news headlines on the page and choose one that looks interesting. (Note: All the sites in Box 20 have an extra sentence that summarises each news report before you click to look at the full article.)

2   Before they click the link to open the full article, tell them that they will have three minutes to read the article. If they come to an unknown word

they should just ignore it and continue reading. If the article is long, they should just read a few paragraphs from the beginning and the end. Then they click and start reading.

Box 20   Business news sites on the Internet

http://www.iht.com/business.html
http://news.google.com/news/en/us/business.html
http://news.google.co.uk/news/en/uk/business.html
http://news.bbc.co.uk/1/hi/business/default.stm
http://news.ft.com/business (then choose region)
Look at English-language newspaper websites too

---

3   Ask the students to turn away from the screen and summarise what they have understood from the article in their own words.

Follow-up
This is a nice activity to repeat every lesson with a one-to-one student. As well as leading into a longer and freer discussion, it can also be followed up with work on topic vocabulary from the article.

6.5 Internet translation tools

Focus	Familiarising students with online resources for translation
Level	Elementary – Advanced
Preparation	Set up two or three translation sites in your Favorites/Bookmarks folder. Try typing 'translation tool' into a search engine to see what is available. Some suggested sites are given in Box 21.
Note	Needs one computer per student; particularly suitable for one-to-one. Familiarise yourself with how the tools work before you use them with students. You specify source language and target language and then type in the word or phrase. Experiment to see how well the tool works with single words, then more specialised business vocabulary, and then short phrases like *Can I have a receipt, please?*

Procedure
1   Tell the students that there are various online resources to help them with translation. You are going to look at a few.
2   With your students, choose some vocabulary **from their own languages:** one general word, one specialised business word, and one or two short phrases used in business.

3 Type the words into the different translation tools and compare how they are translated into English.

Box 21   Internet sites with translation tools

http://dictionary.reference.com/translate/text.html
http://babelfish.altavista.com
http://www.freetranslation.com/
http://www.onelook.com/

Follow-up
Repeat, but this time choose vocabulary in English and try translating it into the student languages.

Variation
You can do a similar activity to help students with online resources for grammar and vocabulary practice. To find the sites to look at and compare, type 'English practice' or 'English grammar practice' or 'English vocabulary practice' into a search engine. Some suggested sites:

http://www.better-english.com/exerciselist.html
http://www.englishclub.com
http://www.english-zone.com

And for Business English: http://www.besig.org/links.htm

6.6 Researching your own culture

Focus	Using the Internet to discover information about countries
Level	Intermediate – Advanced
Preparation	Students need to be in front of a computer, looking at one of the sites in Box 22.
Note	Needs one computer per two students. Familiarise yourself with how these sites work before you do the activity with students. You want them to be able to find a short, interesting text that gives some background information about their own country.

Procedure

1 Ask the students to find their own country in the menu, and then to find a short text that introduces some aspect of their country.

2 Ask the students to read the text, and then ask them what they think about it: Is it a good summary? Is there anything they would change? If they could add one thing, what would it be?

3 At the end of the discussion, point out that the Internet is a very useful tool for finding information about countries. Students can research information before going to a country, or before meeting a visitor from another country.

Box 22   Internet sites with country profiles

http://www.lonelyplanet.com/destinations
http://travel.roughguides.com/destinationshome.html
http://www.executiveplanet.com
http://www.cia.gov/cia/publications/factbook
http://www.economist.com/countries

Variations
• Students research other countries that they are interested in.
• Students use information from the sites above to write a short report about their chosen country.

Business topics: cultural awareness

7.1 Cultural controversy

Focus	Introducing inter-cultural issues
Level	Intermediate – Advanced

Procedure

1 Tell students that you are going to write up on the board a statement about culture. You want them to say whether they agree or disagree. You want their immediate reactions, without thinking. They must take a position – they are not allowed to say 'It depends . . .'.

2 Write up on the board **one** of the statements in Box 23.

Box 23   Statements for cultural controversy

All over the world, wherever you go, people are the same.
Globalisation means that there is now only one business culture.
When in Rome, do as the Romans do.
I don't think about cultural differences – I treat everyone I meet as an individual.
Cultural stereotypes are a dangerous thing.
Business is business all over the world – cultural awareness is not that important.

---

3 The whole class discusses the statement: if they agree or disagree, etc.

7.2 Iceberg or onion?

Focus	Discussing inter-cultural awareness
Level	Intermediate – Advanced

Procedure

1 Write on the board, or photocopy and distribute, the question and diagrams in Box 24.

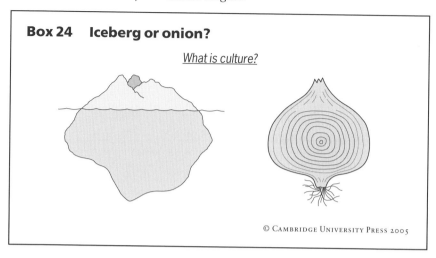

Box 24 Iceberg or onion?

<u>*What is culture?*</u>

© Cambridge University Press 2005

2 Say to the students:

'*Some people think that culture is like an iceberg, other people think that it is like an onion. If culture is like an iceberg, what is below the water and what is above? If culture is like an onion, what are the different layers?*'

3 Ask students to discuss the questions in pairs or small groups for 1–2 minutes.

4 Share ideas with the whole class.

Follow-up

In Box 25 there is a suggested 'answer' that the teacher can explain orally or fill in on the board diagram at the end. Notice that you might need to draw a second onion on the board (the second onion below is more 'businessy').

Box 25 Possible answer to what the iceberg and onion represent

Iceberg	Above the water (what you see) – behaviour, customs, language, dress, music, food, etc. Below the water (what you don't see) – values, attitudes, beliefs
Onion layers 1	(starting from the inside) self, family, gender/age, social class/ethnic group, region/country, universal human nature
Onion layers 2	(starting from the inside) self, team/department, profession, organisation, national culture, international business culture

(And the roots of the onion: history)

In Box 26 there are some ideas to feed into a follow-up discussion.

Box 26   Ideas for follow-up discussion to 'Iceberg or onion?'

Iceberg discussion – It's relatively easy to think of how behaviour and customs differ from one country to another (top of the iceberg), but how do values and beliefs differ? (Possible answers: attitudes to time; directness vs. indirectness; facts and figures vs. personal relationships; competitive/individualistic vs. cooperative/collectivist; hierarchical power structure vs. flat, etc.)

Onion discussion – Is it true that international business culture is becoming the same all over the world? How important are the other layers of the onion: national culture (American business culture vs. European? Chinese vs. Japanese?); professional culture (marketing people vs. finance people?); company culture (Has anyone worked for two companies in the same area of business? How were the cultures different?); gender culture (Do women all over the world have a similar business style?); age culture (Do young people all over the world have a similar business style?), etc.

7.3 Flight to Rubovia

Focus	Discussing inter-cultural awareness
Level	Intermediate – Advanced
Preparation	Write on the board the text in Box 27.

Procedure

1 Say to the students:

> '*You are on your first business trip to Rubovia. You board the flight and the cabin crew and passengers are all speaking Rubovian. You don't understand a word. A Rubovian business person sits next to you and wishes you good afternoon in excellent English. Over the next few hours you have a wonderful opportunity to find out about Rubovian culture, both general culture and business culture. What questions will you ask the friendly passenger at your side?*'

2 Students write down 2–3 questions about general culture, and 2–3 about business culture.

3 The students read out their questions to the class.

Box 27   Flight to Rubovia

Flight to Rubovia

General culture   ┊   *Business culture*

Follow-up

In a mixed nationality class, students can ask and answer the questions.

Variation

As students read out their questions, write them all on the board, reformulating any language errors as you go. Then as a class students discuss which would be the six best questions to ask if there wasn't much time on the flight to have a long conversation.

7.4 Dos and Don'ts

Focus	Discussing how to behave in other cultures
Level	Elementary – Advanced
Preparation	Write on the board, or photocopy and distribute, the text in Box 28.

Procedure

1   Refer to the text in Box 28. Give a few examples, talking about a country you are familiar with. Here are some examples about the UK:

It's worth knowing that England isn't the same as Britain.
Don't be surprised if someone suggests splitting the bill after a meal in a restaurant.
Whatever you do, don't push into a queue. ('cut into line' – American English)

2   As a whole-class activity, elicit ideas to finish the sentences. Students can refer to their own countries, or other countries they are familiar with.

Box 28   Dos and Don'ts

In . . . (name of country) . . .
It's worth knowing that . . .
Don't be surprised if . . .
Whatever you do, don't . . .

Follow-up
Continue the discussion to explore any interesting differences between cultures that come up.

8 Business communication skills: telephoning

8.1 Taking a message

Focus	Practising phone calls
Level	Elementary – Intermediate

Procedure

1 Write on the board, or photocopy and distribute, the phone dialogue structure in Box 29.

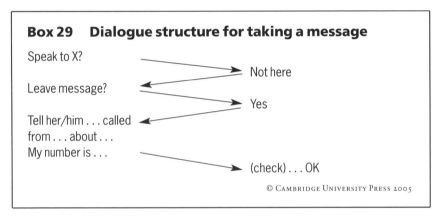

Box 29   Dialogue structure for taking a message

Speak to X?

Leave message?

Tell her/him . . . called
from . . . about . . .
My number is . . .

Not here

Yes

(check) . . . OK

© Cambridge University Press 2005

2 Quickly elicit the lines of the dialogue, but students should **not** write them down (see a possible version in Box 30).

3 Divide the students into pairs and ask them to sit back-to-back and hold up real or imaginary mobile phones to their ears. Tell students that the caller should leave a real message and the receiver should write down the details. Do the role play.

Follow-up

Students do the same activity again, but with a new partner. This time clean the board so they don't have any help.

40

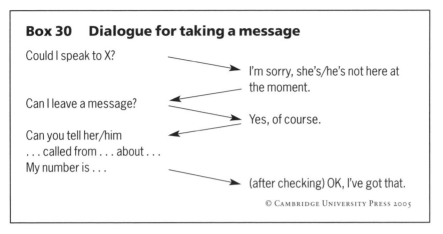

Box 30   Dialogue for taking a message

Could I speak to X?

I'm sorry, she's/he's not here at the moment.

Can I leave a message?

Yes, of course.

Can you tell her/him
. . . called from . . . about . . .
My number is . . .

(after checking) OK, I've got that.

© CAMBRIDGE UNIVERSITY PRESS 2005

8.2 Arranging a meeting

Focus Practising phone calls
Level Elementary – Intermediate

Procedure

1 Write on the board, or photocopy and distribute, the phone dialogue structure in Box 31.

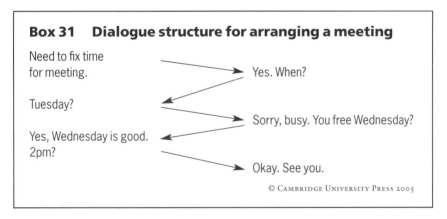

Box 31   Dialogue structure for arranging a meeting

Need to fix time
for meeting.

Yes. When?

Tuesday?

Sorry, busy. You free Wednesday?

Yes, Wednesday is good.
2pm?

Okay. See you.

© CAMBRIDGE UNIVERSITY PRESS 2005

2 Quickly elicit the lines of the dialogue, but students should **not** write them down (see a possible version in Box 32).
3 Divide the students into pairs and ask them to sit back-to-back and hold up real or imaginary mobile phones to their ears. Do the role play.

41

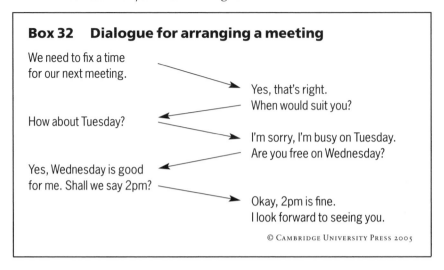

Box 32   Dialogue for arranging a meeting

We need to fix a time for our next meeting.

Yes, that's right.
When would suit you?

How about Tuesday?

I'm sorry, I'm busy on Tuesday.
Are you free on Wednesday?

Yes, Wednesday is good for me. Shall we say 2pm?

Okay, 2pm is fine.
I look forward to seeing you.

© CAMBRIDGE UNIVERSITY PRESS 2005

Follow-up

Students do the same activity again, but with a new partner. This time clean the board so they do not have any help.

8.3 Hotel reservation

Focus Practising short telephone calls
Level Elementary – Intermediate

Procedure

1   Write on the board:

   single room   two nights   Internet   fitness centre   near airport

2   Divide the students into pairs, and allocate roles: the caller (who wants to book a room at a hotel) and the receiver (the hotel receptionist). Ask the students to sit back-to-back and hold real or imaginary mobile phones up to their ears.

3   Tell the students that they should role play a short telephone call where one student reserves a room at a hotel. The caller must use all the words on the board during the call.

Follow-up
Do language feedback, then students repeat the call with a different role
and/or partner.

8.4 Swapping email addresses and phone numbers

Focus	Intensive listening and checking information
Level	Elementary – Intermediate

Procedure

1 Tell the students they are going to exchange business email addresses and
   phone numbers, as they would during a telephone call. They will have to
   write down their partner's details and check carefully that everything is
   correct.

2 Before you start the activity, elicit or pre-teach:

   at for @
   dot in an email address (many students say *point*)
   dash for – (sometimes *hyphen* in British English)
   underline for _ (sometimes *underscore* in British English)
   upper case for ABC
   lower case for abc

3 Divide the students into pairs and ask them to sit back-to-back and hold
   up real or imaginary mobile phones to their ears. Do the activity.

4 Give feedback on areas such as: the importance of pausing after every
   two or three numbers to allow time for the other person to write them
   down; phrases for asking for repetition (*Could you repeat that, please*
   instead of *Can you repeat*); using *zero* in place of the potentially
   confusing *oh* of British English, etc.

Follow-up
Students do the same activity again, but with a new partner.

8.5 Is that N for November?

Focus Clarifying spelling over the phone
Level Elementary – Advanced
Preparation Make a copy of the Spelling Alphabet in Box 33 as an overhead transparency or a handout for the students.

Box 33 Spelling Alphabet

A	Alpha	N	November
B	Bravo	O	Oscar
C	Charlie	P	Papa
D	Delta	Q	Quebec
E	Echo	R	Romeo
F	Foxtrot	S	Sierra
G	Golf	T	Tango
H	Hotel	U	Uniform
I	India	V	Victor
J	Juliet	W	Whisky
K	Kilo	X	X-ray
L	Lima	Y	Yankee
M	Mike	Z	Zulu

© CAMBRIDGE UNIVERSITY PRESS 2005

Procedure

1 Ask students to give a few examples of names of people, products or companies that are often misspelt.
2 Show students the Spelling Alphabet and demonstrate how it can be used to check any spelling that is not obvious.
3 Divide students into pairs and ask them to sit back-to-back.
4 Ask each student to say 1–2 names for their partner to write down. First they should say the whole name, and then they should spell it letter by letter.

8.6 Noisy telephone conversations

Focus	Checking, repeating and summarising information over the phone
Level	Elementary – Intermediate

Procedure

1   Tell students they are going to practise a telephone conversation under difficult conditions. Divide them into pairs, and then ask all the A students to stand with their backs against one wall, and all the B students to stand with their backs against the opposite wall. Make sure that they know who their partner is.

2   Explain the activity: student A is going to call student B to arrange to meet one evening the following week. They will need to discuss the day, time, place, and what they want to do. All the pairs will be talking at the same time, so they will need to check carefully what the other person said and confirm the details at the end. (You can introduce an element of fun by asking the students to use real or imaginary mobile phones and hold them up as if they were really calling.)

3   Remind the students how to begin: student B picks up the phone and says *Hello, X speaking*. Go over to the A students' wall, look at the B students, and start the activity by making the sound of a phone.

4   Give the students a minute at the end of the process to get together quietly and check they understood each other!

Follow-up

You will almost certainly need to look at expressions for checking understanding, e.g. *Sorry, did you say . . . ?*

Business communication skills: meetings and negotiations

9.1 Opening the meeting

Focus Thinking about how to open a formal meeting
Level Intermediate – Advanced

Procedure

1 Write on the board:

Opening a formal meeting: what does the chairperson have to do and say?

2 Brainstorm ideas with the class for a few minutes, and write them randomly on the board. In Box 34 are some ideas.

Box 34 The chairperson's role at the start of a meeting

Getting everybody's attention
Welcoming everyone and thanking them for coming
Checking everyone has a copy of the agenda and other documents
Mentioning when the meeting has to finish
Mentioning any coffee breaks, where the toilets are, etc.
Introducing new colleagues
Reviewing any tasks done since the previous meeting
Giving background information
Explaining the objectives of the meeting
Referring to the agenda
Asking somebody to introduce the first item

---

3 Ask students to put the ideas on the board into a possible sequence. (Note: The ideas in Box 34 are in a possible sequence, although of course variations are possible.)

Follow-up

For homework, students can write out the script to introduce a real meeting in their company. It doesn't matter if in the real meeting they are not going to be the chairperson, or if the real meeting will not be in English. The point is to practise for any future occasion where they may be chairing in English. In the next lesson they can read out their scripts.

9.2 Discussion flowchart

Focus	Having a structured discussion
Level	Elementary – Advanced
Preparation	Write on the board, or photocopy and distribute, the flowchart in Box 35.

Box 35   Discussion flowchart

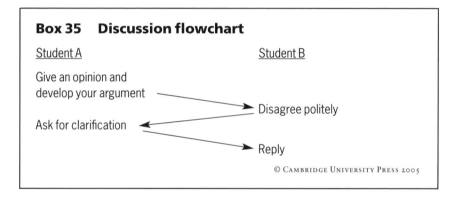

Student A   Student B

Give an opinion and
develop your argument

Disagree politely

Ask for clarification

Reply

© Cambridge University Press 2005

Procedure

1   Brainstorm two or three discussion topics with the class and write them on the board. They can be business or general. In Box 36 are some ideas to feed in if necessary.

Box 36   Discussion topics

The future of Russia/China	Transport problems in cities
Doing business on the Internet	Globalisation
UFOs	Business and the environment
Legalizing soft drugs	The best city in the world
Do advertisements create false needs?	Can we produce enough energy?

And . . . whatever is in the news

---

2   Divide the class into pairs and refer to the flowchart on the board.
3   Ask students to choose a topic and then have a short discussion following the structure on the board.

Follow-up
Do language feedback on the various functions in the discussion: giving an opinion, disagreeing, clarifying.

9.3 The clarification game

Focus	Checking and clarifying information
Level	Elementary – Advanced

Procedure

1   Brainstorm and write on the board a few questions to check or clarify information. For example:

I'm sorry, I don't understand, could you explain that again?
Can you be a little more specific?
What exactly do you mean by 'xxx'?
Are you saying that . . . ?

2   Ask students to write down a one-line statement about their company or business, or a one-line description of their job.
3   Divide students into pairs. Student A reads their statement, then student B asks for clarification, using a question from the board. Student B continues asking for clarification for another five or six turns, forcing student A to explain in more detail and be more specific.
4   Students change roles.

Variation
Other topics for student A's initial one-line statement could be: recent company news, a recent market development, a description of a candidate for a job, a one-line summary of an important decision, or a one-line summary of a recent meeting.

9.4 Disagreeing

Focus	Raising awareness of different ways to disagree
Level	Elementary – Advanced

Procedure

1 Write on the board **one** of these statements, or any similar statement that might amuse or interest the class:

Indian food is the best in the world.
Real Madrid are the best football team in the world.
I think we should move all our production to Vietnam.
Next year we should use Super Audit to audit our accounts.

2 Say the statement aloud and pause for dramatic effect. Tell the students that you want them to think of how they would disagree with you if they heard you say this in conversation. Give them a few seconds to think of something.

3 Go round the group, repeating the statement to each student in turn. Allow them to say their responses.

4 If there is time, repeat for one more statement.

5 At the end review all their phrases and techniques. Some possible ways to disagree are given in Box 37.

Box 37   Techniques for disagreeing

Standard phrase (strong)
I'm sorry, I can't agree with you.
Standard phrase (polite)
I'm not sure I agree with you.
Yes, but
I can see what you're saying, but . . .
Open question
Really? Do you think so?
Negative question
Don't you think that . . .?
Introductory phrase to prepare the listener
Actually, . . .   To be honest, . . .

9.5 Diplomatic language

Focus	Using language that is careful and indirect
Level	Intermediate – Advanced
Preparation	Write on the board, or photocopy and distribute, the text in Box 38.

Box 38   Diplomatic language

There's a problem.

I think there may be a problem with that.
There seems to be a small problem.
Actually, that's not going to be so easy.

© CAMBRIDGE UNIVERSITY PRESS 2005

Procedure

1   Refer to the boardwork. Ask the students what the difference is between the first sentence and the three below. Elicit that the sentences below are more diplomatic/careful/indirect.

2   Tell students that you are going to write up some more short, direct statements. You want them to choose **one**, and then think of different ways to change it so that it has the same meaning but is more diplomatic/careful/indirect. They have three minutes and can work individually or in pairs.

3   Write up a few sentences like those in Box 39, then students do the activity.

Box 39   Direct statements for reformulating in a more diplomatic way

I want to make a change to the agenda.
We can't do that.
Your estimate for the cost is too low.
The project is running late.
That's a stupid thing to say.
The transport costs are very high.
There's a misunderstanding.
There will be a delay.
You're wrong.

---

4   Go round the group and ask them to read out their new sentences.

Follow-up
Do language feedback on the students' use of indirect/diplomatic language.

9.6 Problems, problems

Focus	Making and responding to suggestions
Level	Elementary – Advanced

Procedure
1   Say to the students:

'You have a problem at work. It could be in your office, your department, or your company. It could be with a colleague, your boss, a customer, or a supplier. It could be real or imaginary. What is it? Write it down in a single sentence.'

2   Give the students a minute to think of a problem and write it down.
3   Invite a student to read out their problem. Then all the other students should make suggestions for how to deal with the problem. Anyone in the group can respond to any suggestion.

Follow-up
1   Ask the person who originally read out the problem to choose the best solution.
2   Repeat for other students with other problems.
3   Do language feedback on phrases for making and responding to suggestions. See possible ideas in Box 40.

Box 40   Phrases for making and responding to suggestions

Making a suggestion
Perhaps you could . . .?   Why don't you . . .?   What about . . . (+ -ing)?
Accepting a suggestion
That's a good idea.   That could be worth trying.   What a great idea!
Rejecting a suggestion
I'm not so sure about that.   I can see one or two problems there.

9.7 Crisis!

Focus	Problem solving
Level	Elementary – Advanced
Preparation	Find someone in the company where you teach who knows your students, but is not in the class, e.g. a training manager or secretary that you get on well with. Ask them to think of a possible business crisis that could occur in real life and would affect the work of the students in your group – e.g. a cancelled order, an unexpected delay. Ask them to explain it to you, and not to mention this conversation to your students.
Note	Suitable for in-company lessons only

Procedure

1 Walk into your class and announce the 'crisis' (with a suitable wink if the students take it too literally).

2 Tell students they have four minutes to decide what to do.

Follow-up

Clarify what specific action needs to be taken. Then ask them to perform the tasks they suggest: make telephone calls, write emails, etc.

9.8 Setting the agenda

Focus	Preparing for a meeting
Level	Intermediate – Advanced
Preparation	Select a completed reading text on a **business problem**: an authentic text about a particular company with a problem, or a coursebook case-study.
Note	If using a book, cover up the meeting agenda given in the book.

Procedure

1 Tell the students they are going to hold a meeting to try and solve the problem they have just read about, but first they need to decide on an agenda.

2 Write on the board, or photocopy and distribute, the text in Box 41.

3 Students work in small groups for a few minutes to decide on the items.

4 Ask for their ideas, and if time allows write up an agenda on the board that represents most views/approaches.

Box 41   Setting the agenda

Agenda for Meeting on March 8th

Item 1:
Item 2:
Item 3:

Follow-up
- If using a coursebook case-study, compare with the meeting agenda suggested there.
- Have the meeting. First set a time limit and allocate any roles.

9.9 Negotiation areas

Focus   Preparing for a negotiation
Level   Intermediate – Advanced

Procedure

1   Divide the class into small groups. Tell them that they have just two minutes to brainstorm as many items as possible that a customer and supplier can negotiate about (e.g. *price*). Start the activity.
2   As a round-up, write up all the items on the board. Which group got the most items?

Typical items are: price, discounts, minimum order, terms of payment, delivery time, transport costs, guarantee/warranty, after-sales service, training, installation, maintenance, who pays for advertising, exclusivity in a particular market, specific clauses in the contract such as a penalty clause for late delivery, etc.

Follow-up
- Students explain for their own companies which items are usually negotiable and which non-negotiable (i.e. on which they cannot give a concession).
- For each item, the students say what the typical details or outcomes are for one main product that they sell.

9.10 Firm or flexible?

Focus Discussing negotiation techniques
Level Intermediate – Advanced

Procedure

1   Say to the students:

'In a negotiation, are you firm or flexible? What does it depend on?'

2   Have a whole-class discussion on the issue.

Variation
In Box 42 are some other negotiation issues which you can read out and students can discuss.

Box 42   Negotiation issues

Some people plan a negotiation carefully before they start – they think about their opening positions, their 'bottom line' (beyond which they will walk away), what the other side wants, etc. Other people don't plan in detail – they just wait and see. How much planning do you do before a negotiation?

In a negotiation, are you open and direct, arguing freely with the other side? Or do you prefer to sort out problems quietly and diplomatically, perhaps before or after the meeting?

---

10 Business communication skills: presentations

10.1 Mini-presentations

Focus Giving a demonstration of a presentation
Level Elementary – Advanced
Preparation Choose a topic from Box 43 for a very short presentation of 2–3 minutes that you will give to the students.

Box 43

My country/city
Sales presentation of an article in the room
My current/previous job

Procedure

1 Give the presentation to the students, following the standard structure of a presentation:
   – introduction
   – 2 or 3 points
   – conclusion/summary
   – inviting questions
   The presentation does not have to be particularly good, or funny – just whatever comes. The idea is to show them that you're willing to 'have a go' and so encourage them to, and to show them the standard presentation structure. This is the same whether the talk is three minutes or thirty.

2 Answer a few questions briefly in the remaining two minutes.

Follow-up
Students prepare and give their own short mini-presentations in future lessons. Write up the list of topics above to give them some ideas, but they can choose another topic. Also remind them of the simple structure given above.

10.2 Persuasion

Focus	Giving a mini-sales presentation
Level	Intermediate – Advanced
Preparation	Choose an everyday object in the classroom, perhaps something belonging to a student. It needs to be something with a few features or things to talk about, such as size, colour, packaging, quality. Some suggestions: a bottle of water, a watch, a mobile phone, a dictionary.

Procedure

1 Hold up the object. Tell the students that you want one or two of them to be sales representatives, and the rest of the class will be potential customers. They have to 'sell' the object, i.e. they have to persuade the others that it is the best one on the market, much better than all the competitors. They will have 30 seconds to give their presentations.

2 Allow the students a minute to think of some ideas and make one or two notes, but emphasise that their presentation should be 'heads-up' and without a script.

3 Ask one or two students to give their 30-second presentations. They pass on the object to the next student when they finish.

Follow-up

• At the end, the students can discuss what they liked about their colleagues' presentations – style as well as content.

• In a later lesson, students can present any object of their choice that they have with them.

10.3 Presentation structure

Focus	Discussing the different parts of a presentation
Level	Intermediate – Advanced

Procedure

1 Write up randomly on the board these words:

Examples Recap Bang! Bang! Bridge Message Opening

2 Tell the students that these are different parts of a presentation. Ask them what they think the words mean in this context. Answers (mostly obvious) are given in Box 44.

Box 44   Parts of a presentation

Examples – examples to make your points clear

Recap – short for *recapitulation*, a summary of your main points

Bang! – something that you say or do that has a lot of impact and gets the attention of the audience, e.g. a surprising fact, a reference to 'here and now', a story or joke, audience participation, a visual aid

Bridge – an explanation of how your message connects to the needs of the audience

Message – main points of your presentation (three main points is a good number)

Opening – thanking the organisers for inviting you, a few words about yourself, telling the audience the topic and overall structure of your presentation

---

Follow-up

Ask the students to work in pairs or threes to put the different parts of the presentation into a possible order. There is of course no correct answer and it is interesting for the students to think about, for example, where to put the two *Bang!*s, where to recap, etc. However, one likely answer is:

Bang!   Opening   Message   Bridge   Examples   Recap   Bang!

This makes an easy-to-remember mnemonic using the first letters of the words: *Bomber B*. Giving this mnemonic to the students will help them when they are planning their presentations in the future.

10.4 Signposts

Focus	Eliciting signpost language for a presentation
Level	Intermediate – Advanced
Preparation	Draw a signpost on the board and label it as shown.

Procedure

1   Say to the students:

'When you are on a journey, signposts show the direction you are going, where you are now, and where you have been. What do you think "signposts" are in the context of a presentation?'

2   Elicit the answer, which is that signposts are short phrases that help the
    audience to follow the direction and structure of what you are saying.
3   Elicit a few examples of signpost phrases and write them on the board.
    Some typical phrases are given in Box 45.

Box 45   Examples of signpost phrases

I'm going to talk to you today about . . .   *The point here is . . .*
Let's start by looking at . . .   *Any questions?*
Have a look at this next slide.   *As I said previously, . . .*
Let's move on to . . .   *Finally, . . .*
I'll return to this in a moment.   *So, to sum up, . . .*

Follow-up
•   Photocopy and cut up the individual phrases in Box 46, one set per
    student. There are several ways to use the slips: putting into a possible
    order (the order in the box is one amongst many 'answers'), or making a
    game whereby students have them on the desk and have to use them all
    during a mini-presentation.
•   Remind the students to use some signpost language the next time they
    give a presentation.

Box 46   Signpost phrases to put onto slips of paper

Before I begin I'd like to thank . . . for giving me the chance to talk to you today.

I'm going to talk to you this morning about . . .

I've divided my presentation into three main parts. First . . ., second . . ., and finally . . .

Let's start by looking at . . .

Okay, that's all I want to say about . . .

Any questions so far?

Let's move on to . . .

If you take a look at this next slide, you will see that . . .

Before going on, I'd just like to mention . . .

So, to come back to my main point, . . .

Finally, I'd like to deal with the question of . . .

So, to sum up, I have talked about . . .

Right, let's stop there.

If you have any questions, I'd be pleased to answer them.

© CAMBRIDGE UNIVERSITY PRESS 2005

10.5 To read or not to read, that is the question

Focus Discussing presentation techniques
Level Intermediate – Advanced

Procedure

1   Say to the students:

   '*Some people like to read their presentations word-for-word. Others prefer to use brief notes and speak more freely. What are the advantages and disadvantages of each?*'

2   Have a whole-class discussion on the issue. In Box 47 are some points that are likely to be raised.

Box 47 Reading a presentation word-for-word

Reading word-for-word gives a sense of security to learners of English and they can make sure that it's clear and the audience understands.

But . . . it also means that the speaker will lose eye contact with the audience, the speaker's voice will be less expressive, and generally the presentation might be quite boring.

Follow-up

You can discuss with the class whether there is a compromise. Perhaps this is writing out a presentation in full first, working on it in class and for homework, practising it several times to work on different aspects or different parts, and then giving one 'final' presentation just using notes. If you use slides, then these give a structure and notes aren't necessary.

Variation

In Box 48 are some other presentation issues which you can read out and students can discuss.

Box 48 Presentation issues

Some people like to invite questions from the audience during their presentation. Others prefer to wait until the end. What are the advantages and disadvantages of each?

Some people like to use a lot of PowerPoint slides. Other people prefer to use few visual aids. What are the advantages and disadvantages of each?

Some people like to keep a loose structure to the presentation, interacting with the audience and responding to their questions and interests. Other people like to have a very clear structure with a more formal style. What are the advantages and disadvantages of each?

10.6 The best presentation I ever heard

Focus Discussing presentation techniques
Level Elementary – Advanced

Procedure

1 Ask each student to recall one presentation they heard which they thought was really good. They should note down one reason why it was so good.

2 Share with the whole class and pool ideas on the board.

Follow-up
Do the same for the **worst** presentation they ever heard.

10.7 Effective performance

Focus Giving feedback on performance of a business communication skill
Level Intermediate – Advanced

Procedure

1 After finishing a role play, tell students that for a few minutes you want them to discuss their business performance during the task. If necessary, help them with some prompts:

   – (a presentation) Did they have a good structure to the presentation? Did they keep to the point? Did they reply well to audience questions?
   – (a meeting) Did they explain their opinions simply and clearly? Did they use checking and clarifying when they didn't understand? Was the time in the meeting well used?
   – (a negotiation) Did they listen carefully to the other side? Did they leave options open? Did they summarize if there were a lot of complex points? Did they close the deal well?

2 Divide the students into pairs or small groups and ask them to comment on each other's and their own business performance.

Variation
To give a focus, you could ask each student to think of one thing they consider they did well, and one thing they would like to do better next time.

11 Business communication skills: social English

11.1 First few minutes

Focus Practising small talk
Level Elementary – Advanced
Preparation Choose one specific business situation where a very short period of social English is usual before the 'business' part of the conversation. Some examples are given in Box 49.

Box 49 First few minutes

– on entering the office of a person you are going to negotiate with, before the real business discussion starts
– chatting for a few minutes at the start of a meeting, waiting for people to arrive
– at the beginning of a telephone call, chatting with a colleague from another country who you know well but you haven't seen for some time

---

Procedure

1 Tell the class the situation you have chosen and brainstorm and write on the board topic areas of conversation for this context.
2 Students write a few questions – perhaps one question for each of three topics.
3 Students regroup into pairs or small groups and role play their chat, using the questions they thought of.

Follow-up

After this mini-practice, build the activity into the next full role play that you do. So in the next negotiation/meeting/telephone call begin with some social English before the main business discussion.

11.2 Follow-up questions

Focus Practising conversation for social English
Level Elementary – Advanced

Procedure

1 Brainstorm some discussion topics that are typical in social English (for example while talking in a restaurant). In Box 50 are some ideas to feed in if necessary. Alternatively, photocopy and distribute Box 50.

Box 50   Social English topics

free time interests	business travel
career history	food and drink
comparison of countries	films
sports	families
home towns	holidays
current news items	economic situation
weather	music

© Cambridge University Press 2005

---

2 Divide students into pairs. Explain the activity: student A is to start a conversation by asking B a question about one of the topics, and B will reply. Student A will continue to ask questions, based on B's replies. When A can no longer think of another question, they should make a statement about themselves using a different topic. Student B then starts asking the follow-up questions. In Box 51 is an example, which can be read out to the students.

3 Do the activity.

Box 51   Follow-up questions

A: *How do you relax when you're not working?*   B: *I go to the cinema – I really like films.*

A: *What sort of films do you like?*   B: . . .
A: *What was the last film you saw?*   B: . . .
A: *How often do you go to the cinema?*   B: . . .
A: *Actually, I'm more interested in music.*   B: *Really, what sort of music?*

11.3 Standard exchanges

Focus Reviewing phrases and expressions

Level Elementary – Advanced

Preparation Find a collection of standard exchanges, either question and answer or statement and response, and write them in a grid as shown in Box 52. Alternatively, photocopy Box 52 and cut it up.

Box 52 Lines from exchanges to photocopy and cut up

A gin and tonic, please.	How about 7.30?
Can I borrow your pen?	I'll call you back.
Have a good evening.	Would you like a coffee?
How are you?	Do you mind if I smoke?
Not too bad, thanks.	Actually, I'd rather you didn't.
OK, see you tomorrow.	No, don't bother. I'll do it.
Right, I'm off.	Would you like me to arrange that?
Sure. Here you are.	OK. Speak to you later.
Thanks for all your help.	Would you like to go for a meal later?
What can I get you?	What time shall we meet?
Yes, you too!	Thank you. I'd love one.
You're very welcome.	Thank you. I'd love to.

© CAMBRIDGE UNIVERSITY PRESS 2005

Procedure

The students try to match up phrases to make two-line exchanges. The answers for Box 52 are given in Box 53.

Follow-up

Go on to elicit the functions of the exchanges (e.g. greeting, offering) and brainstorm other phrases and expressions for these functions.

Box 53   Answers to standard exchanges in Box 52

How are you?	$\rightarrow$	Not too bad, thanks.
What can I get you?	$\rightarrow$	A gin and tonic, please.
Do you mind if I smoke?	$\rightarrow$	Actually, I'd rather you didn't.
What time shall we meet?	$\rightarrow$	How about 7.30?
Can I borrow your pen?	$\rightarrow$	Sure. Here you are.
I'll call you back.	$\rightarrow$	OK. Speak to you later.
Right, I'm off.	$\rightarrow$	OK, see you tomorrow.
Would you like me to arrange that?	$\rightarrow$	No, don't bother. I'll do it.
Have a good evening.	$\rightarrow$	Yes, you too!
Would you like a coffee?	$\rightarrow$	Thank you. I'd love one.
Thanks for all your help.	$\rightarrow$	You're very welcome.
Would you like to go for a meal later?	$\rightarrow$	Thank you. I'd love to.

11.4 What do you say when . . . ?

Focus Introducing the language for survival situations
Level Elementary – Intermediate

Procedure

1   Write up on the board:

What do you say when . . . ?

2   Ask students to think of 'survival' situations where they don't know what to say in English or are not sure. They should write down on slips of paper three questions using the sentence head on the board. Some examples are given in Box 54, but it is better if the students think of their own situations.

Box 54   Survival situations

You meet someone for the first time.
The taxi fare is €11.40 and you are happy to give a small tip, but you only have a twenty euro note.
You don't know the way to somewhere.
The bill in the restaurant is obviously wrong.

---

3   Students put their slips of paper into a central 'pool'.
4   Choose one or two and say what you yourself might say in the situation. Ask for other ideas and comment on language and appropriacy.

Follow-up
Keep the slips, and return to them in later lessons, a few at a time, until they are all used up.

11.5 Menus

Focus	Explaining local dishes to a visitor
Level	Elementary – Advanced

Procedure

1   Ask each student to write down on a piece of paper the names of one starter, one main dish and one dessert that might appear on the menu at a local restaurant. The dishes should be national or regional dishes that a visitor would not recognise, and will be written in L1, not English.
2   Divide the students into pairs. Students explain their dishes to their partner, with the partner in role as a visitor who has never heard of or eaten the dishes. Circulate and help with vocabulary for different ingredients, cooking styles, etc. Write up useful vocabulary on the board as you go.

Follow-up
This activity would be a good introduction to a fuller role play 'in the restaurant'. Choose a selection of dishes to write up on the board as the menu for a restaurant (with a humorous name chosen by the students – perhaps Chez Fiona if the teacher is called Fiona). Rearrange the room into restaurant tables and chairs, and group the students into threes or fours. The students all move outside the room, then enter the restaurant group by group to be greeted by the waiter (the teacher), who shows them to their table. They discuss the menu, make their choices, call the waiter to give the order, then make small talk while they wait for the food.

11.6 It's a good story, isn't it?

Focus Telling anecdotes as a skill in social English
Level Elementary – Advanced

Procedure

1 Explain that telling anecdotes and stories is an important part of conversation, and something that can be practised. In this lesson you will tell an anecdote of your own, as example and encouragement.

2 Then tell a short anecdote: something that has happened to you personally, or a famous incident. Encourage them to enjoy understanding an interesting story. You can find business anecdotes at:

http://www.anecdotage.com/browse.php?term=Business

3 Allow a few responses from the students.

Follow-up
Say that you want the students to think of an anecdote of their own to tell in the next lesson, and to practise telling it before the class.

12 Language work: speaking

12.1 'Wh' questions

Focus Getting to know you: question formation
Level Elementary – Intermediate

Procedure

1 Write on the board:

    Who   What   Where   When   Why   How

2 Divide the students into pairs, but do not put them sitting together yet.
3 Give the students two minutes to write as many questions as they can about their partner's job or company. They should write questions that they really want to ask, beginning with the words on the board.
4 After two minutes stop them, get the pairs to sit together, and tell them to ask and answer the questions.

Follow-up

• If you see the activity is going well, allow time for follow-up questions and more discussion.
• Provide language feedback on question forms, if necessary.

12.2 Things in common

Focus Getting to know you
Level Elementary – Advanced

Procedure

1 Put students in pairs or groups and ask them to find three things they have in common that have to do with their jobs, companies, careers, interests, etc.
2 Students report back on the most interesting thing they found.

12.3 Days of the week

Focus Discussing your working (and non-working) life
Level Elementary – Advanced

Procedure

1 Ask students what their favourite day of the week is and why.
2 Then ask them to list the other days in order of preference. Give them
   your own list, for example:

Friday (favourite)
Sunday
Saturday
Thursday
Wednesday
Tuesday
Monday

3 Students pair up and compare and explain their ordering. Encourage
   them to ask each other questions.

Follow-up
Students write a sentence or two for each day of the week, saying why they
like/don't like it, or saying what they typically do on those days.

12.4 Time management

Focus Discussing the working day
Level Elementary – Advanced

Procedure

1 Brainstorm with the class some typical activities in a working day, e.g.
   meetings, telephoning, reports, emails, dealing with customers,
   managing other staff, meals. Write them up on the board.
2 Ask students to write down the approximate time they spend on each
   activity.
3 Students get together in pairs or small groups and compare.

Follow-up
Ask students to write down for each item the time they would like to spend
on that activity in an ideal world. They get together again and think about a

few practical measures that they could take to move a little closer to their ideal world.

Variation

Brainstorm a few extra things that the students don't do at all, but would like to have time for. For example: physical exercise, reading professional magazines to keep up-to-date. How could they find time to do these things?

12.5 My goldfish just died

Focus	Discussing excuses for being late
Level	Intermediate – Advanced

Procedure

1   Write on the board:

My goldfish just died.

Ask students to imagine why somebody might say this at work. Then tell them that it has been used (apparently) as an excuse for being late for work.

2   Ask students to relate other excuses for being late that they have heard or used themselves. Which do they think are and aren't acceptable?

Follow-up

This activity could introduce a discussion about how the company treats (unavoidable) lateness, personal needs, problems, ill-health, etc.

Variation

If you want to feed in some ideas at stage 2, you can find examples on the websites in Box 55.

Box 55   Websites with excuses for being late

http://www.myvirtualreality.co.uk/late.pdf
http://www.members.tripod.com/madtbone/work.htm
http://www.keepersoflists.org/ (type 'late' into search box)

12.6 Current project

Focus	Discussing a special project
Level	Intermediate – Advanced
Preparation	Write on the board, or photocopy and distribute, the text in Box 56.

Box 56   Current project

Current project

Aims:

Resources (material, financial, human):

Progress:

Main problem and possible solution:

© CAMBRIDGE UNIVERSITY PRESS 2005

Procedure

1 Ask students to think of a current project they are working on at the moment: something temporary and different to their normal job. Then ask them to write one sentence for each of the headings on the board.
2 One volunteer uses their notes to give a mini-presentation, followed by questions from the group.

Follow-up
• Other students give their mini-presentations in later lessons.
• The notes are collected in by the teacher and marked. The teacher also writes questions in the margin to prompt the students to think in more depth. (How were these aims decided? Have the aims changed? Where do these resources come from? Will progress continue to be so good? What is holding back progress? How will this solution be implemented?) After receiving the corrected notes and the comments, the students then write a short report on the project.

12.7 Fact or fiction?

> Focus Getting to know you: question formation
> Level Elementary – Advanced

Procedure

1   Write up on the board three statements about your own professional life: one true, one half-true, and one false.
2   Students ask you a few questions about each statement. You give short replies (inventing information where the original was half-true or false).
3   Students work together in pairs or groups to decide which is true, which is half-true and which is false. Then they check with you.

Follow-up
Students write similar sentences about themselves, read them out, and are asked questions by the others, as above. The others pick out the fact from the fiction.

Variation
This also works well with general statements about any aspect of your job, particularly as a Day One 'getting to know you' exercise.

12.8 I'll never forget

> Focus Discussing work experiences
> Level Intermediate – Advanced

Procedure

1   Write up on the board:

   . . . , *and I'll never forget that experience.*

2   Ask a volunteer to tell the group in a few sentences about something that happened to them at work, finishing with the words on the board. If there is time, there can be a question or two.

Follow-up
Invite more volunteers to do the same.

Language work: writing

13.1 Email tips

Focus	Discussing how to write an effective email
Level	Intermediate – Advanced

Procedure

1 Write on the board:

   What advice can you give on how to write an effective email?

2 Brainstorm ideas with the class and write them on the board. In Box 57 are some ideas.

Box 57   Tips for writing effective emails

Use a short, clear subject line.
Use short, simple sentences.
Include just one main subject per email – the other person can reply and delete it.
Don't use jokes, personal comments, etc, in business emails.
Consider using numbered points instead of continuous text.
End with an action point.
Don't ignore capital letters, spelling and basic grammar – when writing to people outside the company a careless email creates a bad impression.
Tailor your email to the reader: level of formality, buzzwords, etc.

Follow-up
This activity would be a good warmer at the start of a series of lessons on email writing. Students can then be encouraged to refer back to the list of tips when they write emails in later lessons, and make any changes necessary as part of the editing process.

13.2 Follow-up email

Focus	Writing emails
Level	Elementary – Advanced

Procedure

Tell the students to write an email following another classroom activity. Set an upper limit of 30 words. For example:

– following a telephone call, to confirm the details
– following a social English role play, to say you enjoyed meeting the other person and perhaps giving them some useful information
– following a Meetings role play, explaining the main points or decisions to a colleague who wasn't at the meeting
– following work on an authentic text. You are emailing a colleague with a copy of the text as an attachment, so write a one-line summary of its content and say why you thought they would be interested.

Follow-up

• Students exchange emails and reply.
• Students correct other students' emails, working in pairs.

Variation

Tell students to write an email of **exactly** 30 words.

13.3 Quick email responses

Focus	Writing a short email
Level	Elementary – Advanced

Procedure

1 Write on the board, or dictate, the following email:

   Still haven't received the goods. Please contact urgently!

2 Ask the students to write an appropriate response to this. They have just three minutes.

3 Students read their responses aloud to the class.

Follow-up

• Discuss with the class which response is best, and why.
• Do language feedback on any phrases or expressions the students needed.

13.4 Chain letter

Focus	Writing a letter or email
Level	Intermediate – Advanced

Procedure

1   Write up on the board:

I am writing to apply for the job of . . .

Ask the students to write this down on a piece of paper, adding a job.

2   Each student then passes their paper to the person on their left, who adds one more sentence. They then pass the paper on again.

3   After several passes, ask students to read out the whole text.

Follow-up
- Do language feedback on any of the standard phrases and expressions.
- Build up a 'collective best version' on the board.

Variation
Try the same activity using the opening phrases below, perhaps as revision after working on the same type of letter in a previous lesson. Many of them are more likely to be emails than letters.

I am writing to arrange a time for . . .
Before I place a firm order, I would like to know . . .
Just a quick note to say many thanks for . . .
I am writing to complain about . . .

13.5 Writing emails

Focus	Writing a short email
Level	Elementary – Advanced
Preparation	Write on the board two or three email topics, relevant to the background/interests of the group. See Box 58 for ideas. Alternatively, photocopy and distribute the text in Box 58.

Procedure

Ask the students to choose one of the topics and write a short email. Give them a word limit of 50 words. As far as possible, they should use ideas from the emails they have to write in real life.

Box 58   Email topics

An email to a real-life company asking about products or services that you are interested in

An email to an existing customer providing information about products or services

An email to a new customer providing information about products or services

An email to a colleague from your department

An email to a colleague from another country

An email to your line manager

An email complaining about products or services

An email replying to a complaint

An email asking for travel or hotel information

An email setting up or cancelling a meeting

An email to a language school, university, etc., asking about details of a course

© CAMBRIDGE UNIVERSITY PRESS 2005

Follow-up
- Exchange emails with a partner. Reply to the email you receive.
- Repeat with another email on another day.

Variation

Rather than write topics on the board, begin by asking the group what real emails they will have to write in the near future. Each student can then practise writing their own email, or you can choose just one of the ideas for the whole group to write their own version.

13.6 Reformulate a letter to an email

Focus Paraphrasing in a different style, summarising
Level Intermediate – Advanced

Procedure

1   Ask students to look at a short business letter in a coursebook. If possible choose one that they are familiar with.
2   Allocate paragraphs round the class, one paragraph per student.
3   Tell students that they have to rewrite their paragraph so that it would be suitable for an email. Explain that the content will be the same, but that the email will be shorter, simpler, more direct and less formal. You could photocopy the example in Box 59 and show it to them first.

Box 59   Example of original letter and reformulated email

Thank you for your letter dated 25 March enclosing a brochure with details of your new range of children's toys. I apologise for not replying sooner, but I have been out of the country on business.

The new range looks very good, and we are particularly interested in your Action Hero figures that we are sure will sell well in our stores. I would be grateful if you could send me some samples, and also a price list with details of any discounts you offer for large orders.

Thanks for your email with the attachment showing your new range. Sorry I haven't been in touch – I've been really busy.

The new products look great – we're very interested in the Action Hero figures. Can you send some samples? And info re prices/discounts?

© CAMBRIDGE UNIVERSITY PRESS 2005

Follow-up
Read out and discuss the answers. Options include:

- a 'collective best version' – build up on the board one possible solution using the best ideas of the group, reformulating as you go.
- looking at each other's versions – perhaps pass round in the group or pin up on the wall – and then make comments on the language and style.

13.7 Email abbreviations

Focus	Recognising common abbreviations used in emails
Level	Elementary – Advanced
Preparation	Write on the board, or photocopy and distribute, the abbreviations in Box 60.

Procedure

1 Tell students that they have three minutes to write down the meaning of as many of the abbreviations as possible. If they don't know, they should move on quickly.

2 Check answers (see Box 61).

Box 60   Email abbreviations

am	e.g.	NB	qty
asap	etc.	pcs	re
btw	FYI	Pls	ref
Bw	i.e.	pm	RSVP
cc	IMO	PS	tbc

© CAMBRIDGE UNIVERSITY PRESS 2005

Box 61   Answers to email abbreviations in Box 60

am – in the morning (*ante meridiem*)
asap – as soon as possible
btw – by the way
Bw – Best wishes
cc – copy to (carbon copy)
e.g. – for example (*exemplii gratia*)
etc. – etcetera
FYI – for your information
i.e. – that is to say (*id est*)
IMO – in my opinion
NB – please note (*nota bene*)

pcs – pieces
Pls – please
pm – in the afternoon (*post meridiem*)
PS – postscript
qty – quantity
re – regarding
ref – reference
RSVP – please reply (*répondez s'il vous plaît*)
tbc – to be confirmed

13.8 Passing notes

Focus Practising functional language in memo writing
Level Elementary – Advanced

Procedure

1   Write on the board the text in Box 62.

Box 62   Types of memos

request   invitation

suggestion   advice   recommendation

---

2 Quickly check that students know the meanings of all the words.

3 Pair up each student with someone who is not sitting next to them. Ask them to choose **one** of the types of communication on the board and write a short note to their partner based on it. Stress that the message doesn't have to be serious!

4 Students write and exchange their notes, and then respond.

Follow-up
Do language feedback on any standard phrases and expressions.

13.9 The purpose of this report

Focus	Dictation as preparation for report writing
Level	Intermediate – Advanced
Preparation	Find a report (coursebook or authentic) that has a short, clear, easy-to-understand introductory paragraph. An example is given in Box 63. Alternatively, find a suitable report and write your own opening paragraph.

Box 63

The purpose of this report is to investigate the management trainees' introductory course in order to determine the reasons for the high failure rate and recommend improvements.

© CAMBRIDGE UNIVERSITY PRESS 2005

Procedure
1 Read out the paragraph as a dictation.
2 Students check with the original opening paragraph (coursebook/handout/board).
3 Use the opening paragraph to brainstorm a possible overall structure for the report.

Follow-up
Brainstorm the vocabulary that might occur in the text, then students actually write the report. At the end they compare with the original report.

Language work: listening

14.1 Dictating news headlines

Focus Intensive listening and note-taking
Level Intermediate – Advanced
Preparation Find 3–4 business or financial headlines from the paper. Avoid any language that is too obscure.

Procedure

1 Dictate the headlines to the students twice, at normal reading speed. Students should write down as much as they can, but reassure them that you don't expect them to get everything.
2 Students check together in pairs or threes to see what they can add to each other's versions. They can ask you to repeat a few headlines, which you do again at normal speed.
3 Write the headlines on the board for the students to check.

Follow-up
• Clarify any relevant areas of vocabulary, connected speech or pronunciation that caused problems.
• Discuss the content of any headlines the students find interesting.

14.2 Jumbled sentences

Focus Intensive listening, discussing how to order sentences
Level Elementary – Advanced
Preparation Find a short coursebook text such as a listening tapescript, a reading text or a letter/email/fax/report. Select an extract from the text where there are 5–6 sentences together, or 5–6 turns together in the case of a tapescript. Write out the sentences onto separate slips of paper. There are examples in Boxes 64 and 65. The sentences in the examples are in the correct order.
Note The whole extract should make sense on its own, but it can be from the beginning, middle or end of the text.

Box 64   Sentences from a tapescript to photocopy and cut up

Can I invite you to have dinner with us this evening?

That would be nice. Thank you.

What kind of food do you like?

Oh, I don't mind. I like all kinds of food.

Oh, well, there are plenty of places to choose from then!

© CAMBRIDGE UNIVERSITY PRESS 2005

Box 65   Sentences from a letter to photocopy and cut up

I am writing with reference to order no. AS 671 which we received last week.

When we checked the machine we noticed some damage to the case and when we turned it on it did not work.

It seems that the machine was not packed properly or tested before shipping.

Please let us know what you intend to do about this matter.

I look forward to hearing from you soon.

© CAMBRIDGE UNIVERSITY PRESS 2005

Procedure

1 Divide the students into groups of 5–6: the same as the number of sentences/turns you have prepared. Distribute the slips of paper randomly.

2 The students in each group read out their sentences to each other.

3 Tell them that you want them to sequence the text. They can read their sentences out to the others as often as they want, discuss, etc. However, they cannot show their piece of paper to anyone, or look at anyone else's.

4 When they have finished, they lay out the slips of paper on a desk in their chosen order.

81

Follow-up
Look back at the original text to check. If it is a listening tapescript, play the extract.

Variation
If you have two or three groups with 5–6 students in each group, then you can use consecutive extracts from the same text. In this way you could prepare, study or revise most or all of a short text.

14.3 Stop the tape and continue

Focus	Reconstructing a listening text
Level	Elementary – Advanced
Preparation	Find a coursebook listening activity with two speakers, such as a telephone call. Choose one for which you have already done all the listening comprehension exercises so that students are familiar with the dialogue.

Procedure
1   Tell the students that you are going to play the tape one more time, but that this time you are going to stop it halfway through. They will continue themselves. They can speak the rest of the dialogue sticking closely to the original, or improvise a few changes if they want to.
2   Divide the class into pairs and make sure that students know which is their role. Do the activity.

Follow-up
Some pairs can act out their continuations for the class.

Variation
Tell the students a small but important change that will affect the outcome of the dialogue.

14.4 Incorrect summaries

Focus	Intensive listening
Level	Intermediate – Advanced
Preparation	Select a completed reading or listening task.

Procedure
1   Tell students to close their books and say that you are going to summarise the text they have just been working on. However, you are going to

change a few details. If they hear something different, they should stop you.

2 Do the activity: briefly summarize the text in your own words, changing 4–5 details. Students stop you as you go along and correct what you have just said.

14.5 Listen and count

Focus	Review of lexical expressions
Level	Elementary – Intermediate
Preparation	Choose 5–8 expressions that students have seen and studied in previous lessons.

Procedure

1 Tell students you are going to read out some expressions they will recognise. They should listen and write down the number of words in each. Contracted forms (I'm, don't) count as two words.

2 Do the activity. Make sure you read the expressions fluently and naturally, with natural word-linking as you would in normal speech.

3 Students compare their answers in pairs and then check with you.

Follow-up

• Read out the expressions again, but this time students write down the whole expression as a dictation. They compare their answers in pairs while you write up the expressions on the board.

• Ask students to think of other expressions for the same situation (either remembering previous lessons, or perhaps thinking of new expressions).

15 Language work: reading

15.1 Response to a text

Focus	Giving a quick personal response to a reading text
Level	Intermediate – Advanced
Preparation	Start with any completed reading activity – coursebook or authentic source – where you want students to move into a discussion of the main issues rather than doing comprehension exercises or checking unknown vocabulary.
Note	This activity works particularly well after students have read an article for homework.

Procedure

1   Write on the board, or photocopy and distribute, the headings in Box 66.

Box 66   Response to a text

Something that surprised me
Something that interested me
Something I'm not sure about
Something I'd like to ask the other members of the class

© Cambridge University Press 2005

---

2   Ask students to write a sentence for each heading with their own responses to the text.

3   Ask one student to read out their four completed sentences and move into a short class discussion.

Follow-up
Continue with other students' responses and more discussion.

15.2 Questioning the text

Focus Introducing a short text by asking questions
Level Elementary – Advanced

Procedure

1 Before a reading or listening activity, tell students the topic of the text. If it has a headline or title, write it on the board.
2 Ask students what questions they hope the text will answer. Take a minute to brainstorm the questions and write them on the board.
3 Students read or listen to the text to check which questions are and aren't answered.

Variation

Ask students what words they think will come up in the text. Brainstorm and write them on the board, then check with the text, as above.

15.3 More than single words

Focus Dealing with vocabulary in a text
Level Elementary – Advanced

Procedure

1 Following a reading task, ask the students to choose five key words from the text, which you write on the board.
2 Refer to the first occurrence of the words, and ask the students to 'look left and right of the word' and shout out the collocations for you to write up.
3 Continue for other occurrences of the same words, and their collocations.

Follow-up

Students summarise the text using the collocations on the board.

15.4 Figures in the news

Focus Finding key information in a text
Level Elementary – Advanced

Procedure

1 Dictate 3–4 figures (numbers, percentages, amounts of money, etc.) from a business news text that you are going to study or discuss later.
2 Ask students to work in pairs and check they have written down the same figures.
3 Hand out the text. Tell students that they have two minutes to find the figures and discover what they refer to.

15.5 Class-generated text summary

Focus Introducing a text through summarising
Level Elementary – Advanced

Procedure

1 Before a reading or listening activity, tell students the topic of the text. If it has a headline or a title, write it on the board.
2 Ask students to look at the text. Go round the group, allocating one paragraph per student (in order, according to how they are seated).
3 Tell students that they have just two minutes to write a one-sentence summary of their paragraph. They should use simple language, and should avoid words from the original that other students might not understand. They can ask you for help.
4 When the students are ready, they read out their sentences, in order, round the group.

Follow-up

• Ask students to read their sentences in order around the group one more time. Then divide the students into pairs and ask them to try to remember and retell the whole summary.
• Move into a discussion of the content of the article, or use the text for language work (perhaps looking for topic-related vocabulary).

Language work: pronunciation

16.1 Phonological chunking

Focus	Raising awareness of speech patterns (phonological chunks/tone units)
Level	Elementary – Advanced
Preparation	Find a short extract from a listening text that the students are familiar with, and for which you have an audio recording. Write it on the board. See the example in Box 67.
Note	The text needs to be a monologue, composed of several separate utterances, and lasting about 20 seconds.

Box 67   Extract from a listening text

Tai Chi is not Kung Fu or anything like that. The idea of Tai Chi is very different, it's internal. There are four main elements: firstly, working on the way we breathe; secondly, our body position; thirdly, learning soft movements to help energy and balance; and the final element is meditation, a quiet part, which many people like.

© CAMBRIDGE UNIVERSITY PRESS 2005

Procedure

1   Ask the students to look at the text on the board and try to decide where the speaker would pause. This will always be at the end of a sentence, but can be in the middle as well, perhaps several times. Emphasise that there is no 'right' answer, and that fluent speakers would pause differently on different occasions with the same text.

2   Elicit possible answers and write on the board, drawing a diagonal line where a pause is possible. Read the sentences aloud yourself as you go, with the pauses the students suggest, to see if you/they feel it is natural.

In Box 68 there is a possible chunked version of the text in the first box, with prominent syllables marked (as discussed in the Follow-up).

Box 68   The same text as Box 67, with chunks and prominent syllables marked

Tai **Chi** / is **not** Kung **Fu** /or **any**thing like **that**. / The **idea** of Tai **Chi** / is very **different**, / it's in**ter**nal. / There are **four main** elements: / **first**ly, / **work**ing on the way we **breathe**;/ **sec**ondly, / our **bod**y position;/ **third**ly, / learning **soft movements** / to help **energy** and **bal**ance;/ and the **final** element / is medi**ta**tion, / a **quiet** part, / which **many** people **like**.

Follow-up

• Play the extract on the tape and get them to compare with what is on the board.

• Students practise saying the extract themselves, paying attention to the phonological chunking.

• After this, discuss with the students which would be the prominent syllables inside each chunk. Underline them. Then practise:
a) first provide a model by saying the statements yourself, beating with your hand to show the strongly stressed syllables;
b) now ask students to repeat each statement chorally after you;
c) finally ask students to practise by themselves, building up to saying the whole extract with appropriate stress and pausing.

16.2 Stress patterns

Focus Awareness of rhythm and stress
Level Elementary – Advanced
Preparation Start with the board full of a mixture of complete sentences, phrases, collocations and single words. This could be left over from language feedback following a speaking activity, or a list of recently-learnt vocabulary, etc.

Procedure

1 Pick out several phrases and expressions on the board. Ask students to say them to themselves and write down the stress pattern, e.g.
Do you agree? / o o o O /

2 When students are ready, ask them to compare together in pairs before doing feedback with the whole group.

Follow-up
Choose some of the phrases and expressions to practise fluent
pronunciation. This might include work on linking (a sound at the end of
one word links with one at the beginning of the next), elision (a sound is
missed out in normal speech), or intonation patterns (identifying the main
stress and the movement of the voice up and down).

16.3 Problem sounds

Focus Noticing L1/L2 pronunciation differences
Level Elementary – Advanced
Preparation Start with the board full of a mixture of complete sentences, phrases,
collocations and single words. This could be left over from language
feedback following a speaking activity, or a list of recently-learnt
vocabulary, etc.

Procedure
1 Tell the students that you are now going to focus on pronunciation. Circle
several syllables that contain vowel sounds you have noticed students have
difficulty with. Ask students to say the sound. Help them by, for example:
   – asking if the sound is short, long, or a double sound (diphthong).
     For example: *bill* /ɪ/ = short, *fee* /iː/ = long, *time* /aɪ/ = double sound
   – showing them with your mouth how the sound is physically formed.
2 Do some repetition (choral drilling) to give students a chance to practise
making the sound.
3 Ask them to find other words on the board with the same sound.

Follow-up
• Use exercises on minimal pairs (pairs of words where only one sound is
  different). Work on students' ability both to recognise the different sounds
  (teacher says the words and students say which one they heard) and produce
  them (teacher points to words on board and students chorally say them).
• Encourage students to keep a list of problem sounds, noting the different
  spellings of the same sound.

17.1 What's the difference?

Focus	Introducing a business topic
Level	Intermediate – Advanced

Procedure

1 Write 2–3 words or concepts on the board that are similar in meaning but are not quite the same. Choose words from the business topic that you are going to look at in the lesson. See examples in Box 69.

2 Students have to try to explain the difference between the two words. (A dictionary will help if they get stuck.)

Box 69   Pairs of words with similar meanings

marketing/sales	cultural behaviour/cultural values
revenue/earnings	The Board/senior management
advertising/promotion	management/leadership
transport/logistics	performance-related pay/bonus
finance/accounting	gross profit/net profit/retained profit
cheap/value-for-money	information technology/e-business
research/innovation	target/objective
wholesaler/retailer	fire/lay off
health/safety	customer/client

17.2 Brainstorming collocations

Focus	Introducing vocabulary of management (or other business topics)
Level	Intermediate – Advanced

Procedure

1 Write up on the board the keyword *management*.

2   Ask students to suggest words that collocate with the keyword. Remember the different types of collocation, e.g. adjective + keyword, verb + keyword, noun + keyword, keyword + noun. Some examples have been given in Box 70 to help you.

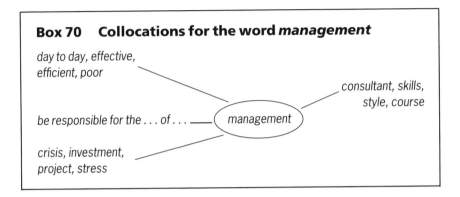

Box 70   Collocations for the word *management*

day to day, effective,
efficient, poor

consultant, skills,
style, course

be responsible for the . . . of . . .   management

crisis, investment,
project, stress

Follow-up
Get students to compare collocations with their L1 noting similarities and differences.

Variation
Do the same for other keywords. Most dictionaries now provide collocations which will give you ideas to feed in, and there are also specialist collocation dictionaries. There is another example in Box 71.

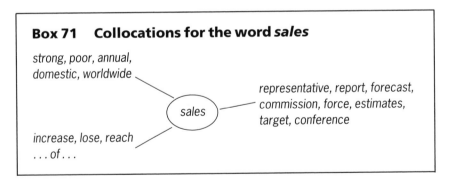

Box 71   Collocations for the word *sales*

strong, poor, annual,
domestic, worldwide

representative, report, forecast,
commission, force, estimates,
target, conference

sales

increase, lose, reach
. . . of . . .

17.3 Devowelled words

Focus Reviewing vocabulary of any business topic
Level Elementary – Advanced

Procedure

1 Choose 6–7 key terms around a business topic which students have learnt and need to review, and write up the words without vowels. The following example list comes from the topic of *marketing*:

prmtn   mssg   cmmrcl   slgn
dvtsmnt   brnd   trgt cstmr

Answers: promotion, advertisement, commercial, slogan, message, brand, target customer

2 Tell students the topic and ask them to work out the words.
3 Go through the list with the class, checking understanding and spelling.

Follow-up
To develop the students' ability to use the words, brainstorm or use a collocation dictionary to make a short list of words that collocate with the key terms. Students can then write sentences using the collocations.

17.4 Lexical dominoes

Focus Reviewing collocations and expressions of marketing (or any other topic)
Level Elementary – Advanced
Preparation Before the lesson, select 15–20 collocations or phrases that have come up in recent lessons, and write them in a grid as shown. Examples for the topic 'marketing' are shown in Boxes 72 and 73. The beginning of the collocation or phrase is written on the right of one domino, the end is written on the left of the next domino. Copy the grid and cut it into horizontal strips to make one set of dominoes for each group of students.

Procedure

Hand out the sets of dominoes to small groups. Students play the game: they try to lay out the dominoes end to end on the table.

Box 72	Dominoes for 'the marketing mix'	
(Start)	◆	marketing
mix	◆	retail
outlet	◆	word
of mouth	◆	target
customer	◆	market
leader	◆	main
competitor	◆	selling
point	◆	value
for money	◆	point
of sale	◆	income
bracket	◆	niche
market	◆	share
of the market	◆	(Finish)

Box 73	Dominoes for a presentation on marketing	
(Start)	◆	increase
our market share	◆	Please feel
free to interrupt	◆	carry out
a market survey	◆	Let's start
by looking at . . .	◆	an emerging
market	◆	The trend
seems to be towards . . .	◆	our full product
range	◆	Let's now
move on to . . .	◆	I'd like to go back
for a moment to . . .	◆	Right, let's
stop there	◆	We're experiencing
an economic boom	◆	Do you have
any questions?	◆	(Finish)

17.5 What does that stand for?

Focus Recognising business abbreviations
Level Elementary – Intermediate

Procedure

1 Write up on the board three common abbreviations used in business. Some possibilities are shown in Box 74.

Box 74   Business abbreviations

USP	MBA	CEO	VIP
M&A	VAT	IBM	P&L
GDP	PLC	R&D	AGM

These stand for: Unique Selling Point, Mergers and Acquisitions, Gross Domestic Product, Master of Business Administration, Value Added Tax, Public Limited Company, Chief Executive Officer, International Business Machines, Research and Development, Very Important Person, Profit and Loss, Annual General Meeting.

2 Introduce the question *What does X stand for?* Ask students to explain the three abbreviations.

3 Ask students to come to the board and write up a common abbreviation they use in business and ask the other students if they know what it stands for.

Follow-up

- Write up on the board any new vocabulary that individual students needed as they explained their abbreviation.
- Use the opportunity to review letters of the alphabet.

17.6 Hot seat

Focus Reviewing vocabulary
Level Elementary – Intermediate

Procedure

1 Put a chair in front of the board, facing away from the board and towards the class.

2   Ask a student to come up and sit on the chair. You write up on the board a series of language items to be reviewed, one by one. For example:

retained profit
assets
depreciation

Or if you were reviewing telephoning language you might write up these, one by one:

Speaking.
I'm sorry, I didn't catch that.
Would you like to leave a message?

3   The other students have to make the person on the chair say the exact words written on the board. They do this by giving hints: a context when you say the word(s), another way of saying the same thing, a definition, an example, etc. They cannot, however, say any of the words on the board.

4   When a student guesses the item, another student takes the seat and you write up another word or phrase.

Note: You may have to join in if the student on the hot seat is close to guessing but the others cannot think of a way to get them to say the exact words.

17.7 Dictionary search

Focus	Reviewing vocabulary of a business topic
Level	Intermediate – Advanced
Preparation	Make sure you have some English/English student dictionaries in the classroom. These may be general dictionaries or specialised Business English ones.
Note	The activity works well if you have different dictionaries available.

Procedure

1   Write up on the board 3–4 key words related to a business topic that you have recently looked at. Explain that students will look up the words in their dictionaries: not to check their meaning, but instead to check how the words are used. This will mean looking for the **example sentences** and noticing **useful collocations** that they find there.

2 Students use their dictionaries to check the key words, then pool with the whole group what they have found from the example sentences. It is important that you as a teacher also look up the words with the students to be able to answer any questions they may have.

Follow-up
Collect the collocations on the board and explore them with students. You might look at what other words (synonyms, opposites, other collocates) could be substituted as one of the components of the collocation.

17.8 Categorising vocabulary

Focus | Reviewing vocabulary of business topics
Level | Intermediate – Advanced
Preparation | Write on the board, or photocopy and distribute, a set of words around **different** topic areas you have taught in previous lessons. An example is given in Box 75.

Box 75   Words to categorise into groups

benefits	cancel	goods	pension
order	recruit	dispatch	appraisal
warranty	apply	consignment	delay
references	resign	freight	promote
fire	invoice	staff	deliver
customs	deadline	discount	relocate

© CAMBRIDGE UNIVERSITY PRESS 2005

Procedure

1 Ask students to categorise the items according to topic. It is more interesting if you don't tell them what the possible topics are – let them think of their own ways to categorise.
2 Students compare with each other. One possible answer for the words in Box 75 is to divide the words into these two categories:

Human Resources: benefits, pension, recruit, appraisal, apply, references, resign, promote, fire, staff, deadline, relocate
International Trade: cancel, goods, order, dispatch, warranty, discount, consignment, delay, freight, invoice, deliver, customs

Note that there will not be a 'right' answer: students may categorise in different ways and words may fit into various categories depending on the context. Discussing this is a part of the activity, particularly for higher level groups. For example, in Box 75 there are a number of words with different meanings (*benefits, customs, promote, order*) as well as other words that could fit both categories of the possible answer above (*deadline, cancel*).

Follow-up
- Ask students to add three more items to each topic.
- Get students to check a few of the key words in a dictionary and notice any other words or expressions they collocate with (these might be listed explicitly in the dictionary or appear in the example sentences).

17.9 English loan words

Focus	Looking at English words in the students' L1
Level	Elementary – Advanced

Procedure

1 Give a few examples of foreign words in English, e.g. *kindergarten, karaoke, kebab*.

2 Students think of English words and expressions that have come into the business world in their own language and that everybody uses and understands. As there may be a large number, you could restrict this to words that have come into their language only recently (perhaps the last few years).

3 Pool their ideas on the board.

Follow-up
- It might be interesting to explore if and how the pronunciation changes when the English word is used in another language.
- Look out for 'false friends', i.e. words that seem to be English, but actually have a different meaning or are different in use (e.g. the German *handy* for mobile phone, or the ubiquitous *shopping* and *camping* where English would use *shopping mall* or *camp site*).

17.10 Business metaphors

| Focus | Understanding idioms and metaphors |
| Level | Intermediate – Advanced |

Procedure

1 Write up on the board three or four business metaphors. Some examples are provided in Box 76.

Box 76   Business metaphors

He's tied up at the moment.
She was completely out of her depth.
Shares have gained ground.
We're in a tight corner.
The company hit the rocks last year.
He came under fire for his decision.

---

2 Clarify the literal meaning of any unfamiliar words, then ask students to guess the metaphorical meaning of the whole expression.

Follow-up

- Compare with students' L1 to see which metaphors translate.
- What business metaphors are common in the students' L1?
- Look for metaphors in future reading texts, and encourage students to guess the meaning from the context.

17.11 Responding to a lesson

| Focus | Reviewing language learnt in the lesson |
| Level | Elementary – Advanced |

Procedure

1 At the end of a lesson, ask students to look back through their notes and select five language items that they have learnt or reviewed this lesson, and plan to use in future. Allow 2–3 minutes for silent reflection.
2 Ask a few students what they have chosen, and deal with any questions.

Note: Students should be encouraged to keep vocabulary notebooks and write down new items in them every lesson to facilitate later review.

18 Language work: grammar

18.1 Putting back the grammar

Focus Looking at different areas of grammar
Level Elementary – Advanced
Preparation Write on the board a short business news item or an extract from a reading text that students are familiar with. Write it with all the 'grammar' taken out, i.e. articles, prepositions, word endings, past tenses. See examples in Box 77 and the original versions in Box 78.
Note You can adjust the difficulty level according to your group.

Box 77   Two texts with the grammar taken out

Many thank your email. Regard report you ask, I need apologise delay. I very busy last week but send it end today. About meeting next week, please you send agenda Jill – she attend. Look forward see you next week. Best wish . . .

Request, we enclose your attention our price list and catalogue. I like take this opportunity draw your attention fact that all our product manufacture complete natural ingredient and that we not utilize any artificial additive whatsoever.

Box 78   Original versions of the texts in Box 77

Many thanks for your email. Regarding the report you asked for, I need to apologise for the delay. I was very busy last week but can send it at the end of today. About the meeting next week, please could you send an agenda to Jill – she'll be attending. Looking forward to seeing you next week. Best wishes . . .

As requested, we enclose for your attention our price list and catalogue. I should like to take this opportunity of drawing your attention to the fact that all our products are manufactured from completely natural ingredients and that we do not utilize any artificial additives whatsoever.

Procedure

1 Explain to the students what you have done. Tell them they have five minutes to 'put back' as much of the grammar as they can. (Note: There is usually more than one way of doing this.)

2 When they have finished, write up or hand out the original.

Follow-up

Review their work, clarifying what is and is not possible and allow students to ask any questions they might have on different aspects of grammar. Finally, ask students to say what they individually found most interesting about the task.

Variation

You can do a similar activity based on a listening text:

1 Choose a very short passage (2–3 sentences) from a coursebook listening activity or authentic off-air recording from the radio. Play it to the students – a couple of times if necessary – and ask them to write down all the important words.

2 Elicit all the nouns, verbs, adjectives, adverbs that the students heard. Write up the root form, for example the stem form of a verb, a noun without an *s* on the end, etc. Leave out all the little words like *the*, *of*, etc. You will finish up with something similar to the examples in Box 77.

3 Ask students in pairs or groups to put the grammar back to make complete sentences.

4 Write up the full text for students to compare. Play the recording again.

18.2 Expanding sentences

Focus Sentence structure
Level Elementary – Advanced

Procedure

1 Write on the board a simple sentence and ask students to suggest 1–3 words to add anywhere in the sentence to give more detail. For example:

The company made a profit.

Students might suggest additions such as:

The textile company made a profit.
The company made a profit of €4 million.

2   Carry on eliciting further additions for another 3–4 minutes. For example:

The textile company, based in Oporto, made a profit.
The company made a profit of €4 million last year.

Follow-up
Repeat with other sentences on another day. For example:

Shares fell.
Sales increased.
The meeting is postponed.
The launch will be delayed.
The Chief Executive resigned.

18.3   Five-minute dictogloss

Focus	Intensive listening, reconstructing a text
Level	Intermediate – Advanced
Preparation	Choose a one-paragraph business news article from an authentic source that contains useful vocabulary and/or useful grammar. There are many available on the websites in Box 79.

Box 79   Websites for short business news articles

http://news.bbc.co.uk/hi/business/default.stm
http://www.iht.com/business.html
http://news.ft.com/business (then select region)
http://news.google.com/news/en/us/business.html
http://news.google.co.uk/news/en/uk/business.html
Look at English-language newspaper websites too

Procedure

1   Explain to the students that you are going to read the paragraph once at normal speed, and that they should note down the key words while you read. They should not write sentences.
2   Do the activity.
3   Ask the students (individually or in pairs) to try to reconstruct as much of the paragraph as possible in four minutes, using their notes.

Follow-up

Write up the correct version on the board. Review any language points that come up.

18.4 English → L1 → English

Focus	Raising awareness of L1 interference problems
Level	Intermediate – Advanced
Preparation	Write down on slips of paper a number of different sentences taken from a Business English coursebook or Business English grammar book.
Note	Only suitable for monolingual classes or classes with pairs of students from the same country.

Procedure

1   Give one slip of paper (= one sentence) to each student. Working individually, they translate their sentence into their language (L1) and write it on another slip of paper.

2   Each student swaps their L1 sentence with a partner (who has worked on a different original). They translate the L1 sentence they have just been given back into English, again writing it on a slip of paper.

3   Students get together and compare the original English sentences with the new English sentences.

Follow-up

Discuss the differences with the class, pointing out the particular problems of L1 interference that the exercise has revealed.

18.5 France/French

Focus	Distinguishing between countries and nationalities
Level	Elementary – Intermediate

Procedure

1   In one minute, brainstorm and write on the board the names of countries where the students do business or have business contacts.

2   Ask the students (working individually or in pairs) to write the adjective that describes the nationality of people coming from each country. Do the first one as an example.

Follow-up

Check the nouns that describe a person who comes from that country. These are often the same as the adjective, but not always. For example:

America	*American*	*an American*
England	*English*	*an Englishman/Englishwoman*
France	*French*	*a Frenchman/Frenchwoman*
Denmark	*Danish*	*a Dane*

18.6 In my office

Focus	Writing about office procedures using modal verbs
Level	Elementary – Advanced

Procedure

1 Write on the board, or photocopy and distribute, the text in Box 80.

Box 80   In my office

In my office, you should always try to . . .
But you don't have to . . .
You can . . .
But you shouldn't . . .
And you definitely mustn't . . .

© CAMBRIDGE UNIVERSITY PRESS 2005

---

2 Ask students to write 1–2 alternatives to complete each sentence.
   Note: You may want to focus on the modals: *don't have to* for something that is optional, *shouldn't* for something that is a bad thing to do, and *mustn't* for the stronger idea of something that is very bad or not allowed.
3 Students share their sentences with a partner as they finish.

Follow-up

Students read out their sentences, explaining in more detail and answering questions. Some of their sentences might lead to an interesting discussion.

18.7   If it was up to me . . .

Focus	Writing about work using conditional sentences
Level	Elementary – Advanced

Procedure

1   Write on the board:

Changes I'd like to make in my work

If I had the time, . . .
If it was up to me, . . .
. . . if it was possible.

2   Ask students to complete the sentence.
(Note that the three phrases all contain the *if* clause of a conditional sentence, but not the result clause. In the heading the students are given a clue that when they write they should begin *I'd* or *I'd like to* but the exercise gives a chance to test whether or not they actually do this.)

Follow-up
Students read out their sentences, explaining and answering questions.

18.8   Correct yourself

Focus	Encouraging student correction of their own output
Level	Elementary – Advanced
Preparation	During a role play or discussion make a note of common errors.

Procedure

1   Write up on the board the whole phrase or sentence exactly as you heard it, including the error. Give students a few seconds to think about how to correct it, but it is important that you do not let them call it out.
2   Offer the student who said the phrase a chance to self-correct, or if you cannot remember then offer it to the group. Give hints if necessary.
3   If students cannot see what the correct form should be, give it yourself.
4   Correct the original on the board. Add further explanation as necessary.
5   Repeat for other errors.

Follow-up
If the class as a whole still has a problem with the error, take time to do some mini-controlled practice of the language item (perhaps with personalised sentences), or refer to a grammar book exercise for homework, or return to it for more focused practice in the next lesson.

19 Exploiting coursebooks

19.1 Revise key phrases

Focus Reviewing key phrases, classifying
Level Elementary – Advanced
Preparation Find a 'Useful Language' list from a coursebook. The list needs to have functional headings with at least two phrases per heading: see the example in Box 81. Write on the board two phrases per function, in jumbled order, but do **not** write the functional headings. Alternatively, photocopy and cut up the phrases in Box 82, which are taken from Box 81.

Box 81 Telephoning phrases

Answering the phone
Good morning, ABC, how can I help you?
Sales Department, Patricia speaking.

Stating reason for call
I'm calling about . . .
The reason I'm calling is . . .

Saying someone is not available
I'm sorry, she's/he's not available at the moment.
Sorry, she's/he's away on business / in a meeting.

Taking a message
Can I take a message?
Would you like to leave a message?

Checking
Sorry, I didn't catch that.
Could you spell your name please?

Making arrangements
When would be a good time?
What about next Tuesday at ten?

Changing arrangements
I'm afraid I can't come on that day.
Sorry. Can we reschedule for another time?

Ending a call
Right, I think that's all. Thanks for your help.
Goodbye and thanks. / Bye for now.

© CAMBRIDGE UNIVERSITY PRESS 2005

Procedure

The students try to work out which phrases go together, i.e. belong to the same functional group. If the students are working with slips of paper they can match them on the desk in front of them.

Box 82   Telephoning phrases for photocopying and cutting up

Can I take a message?	Would you like to leave a message?
Good morning, ABC, how can I help you?	Sales Department, Patricia speaking.
Goodbye and thanks. / Bye for now.	Right, I think that's all. Thanks for your help.
I'm afraid I can't come on that day.	Sorry. Can we reschedule for another time?
I'm calling about . . .	The reason I'm calling is . . .
I'm sorry, she's/he's not available at the moment.	Sorry, she's/he's away on business/in a meeting.
Sorry, I didn't catch that.	Could you spell your name please?
What about next Tuesday at ten?	When would be a good time?

© CAMBRIDGE UNIVERSITY PRESS 2005

Follow-up

Go on to elicit the functional headings and brainstorm other phrases.

Variation

Dictate the phrases initially, in jumbled order, rather than writing them on the board.

19.2 DIY gapfill

Focus Specific vocabulary or grammar
Level Elementary – Advanced
Preparation Take a few paragraphs (e.g. the first few) from a text that the students are familiar with. Write the text on the board, but leaving gaps. Some suggestions are given in Box 83.

Procedure

Refer to the text on the board. Ask students to complete the gapfill.

Box 83   Techniques for gapping

Gap key topic vocabulary, e.g. words from useful collocations
Gap key words of a particular grammatical type, e.g. prepositions or articles
Gap every seventh word.

Variation

Initially, just have gaps on the board and give no additional help. But if the
students need extra help, then after 2–3 minutes you can do one of these:
– write the missing words in jumbled order at the bottom
– write the first letter in the gap.

19.3 Cover it up (two columns)

Focus Extending a coursebook exercise
Level Elementary – Advanced

Procedure

1   Before doing a matching exercise with two columns, students cover up
the words in the right-hand column. See the example in Box 84.

**Box 84   Two-column exercise where right-hand column
            can be covered**

Match the word combinations (1–7) to their definitions (a–f).

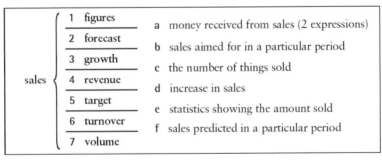

sales {
1 figures
2 forecast
3 growth
4 revenue
5 target
6 turnover
7 volume

a   money received from sales (2 expressions)
b   sales aimed for in a particular period
c   the number of things sold
d   increase in sales
e   statistics showing the amount sold
f   sales predicted in a particular period

© Cambridge University Press 2005

---

2   Students look at the items in the left-hand column and try to predict the right-hand column. Depending on the exercise this might be giving a definition, supplying the second noun of a noun-noun collocation, etc.

3   They uncover the second column and do the exercise as usual.

Follow-up
- In a later lesson, as revision, the teacher reads out the word(s) in the left-hand column item by item. Ask the students to wait five seconds to give everyone time to think, then they give the definition, the collocation, or whatever the exercise requires.
- Alternatively, the students simply cover the right-hand column again and try to remember the matching items.

19.4   Cover it up (gapfill)

Focus   Extending a coursebook exercise
Level   Elementary – Advanced

Procedure
1   Before doing a gapfill exercise, ask students to cover up the words to be used (often in a box) with a piece of paper.
2   They look at the exercise and try to predict possible words that might fill the gaps.
3   Then they uncover the words and do the exercise as usual.

Follow-up
In a later lesson, as revision, the teacher reads out the original exercise containing the gaps again. The teacher says 'Mmm' where the gapped word occurs (but continues reading to the end of the sentence to give a context). Ask the students to wait five seconds at the end to give everyone time to think, then on the teacher's hand signal they chorally shout out the answer.

19.5 Noticing language in a tapescript

Focus	Reviewing vocabulary
Level	Elementary – Advanced
Preparation	Select a completed listening activity.

Procedure

1   Ask students to look at the tapescript. Then:
   a) for business topics, ask them to underline five items of vocabulary related to the topic area; remind them that 'vocabulary' includes more than single words – look for useful collocations too.
   b) for work on communication skills or interactive situations, ask them to underline five useful words or phrases for that particular context.
2   Students compare with partners to see if they underlined the same items.

Follow-up
•   Students write the items on pieces of paper or in their notebooks, then try to use some of them in a following discussion (topic) or role play (communication skill).
•   Students transfer the items to their notebook, with two examples of use:
    i) the item in its original sentence in the tapescript to show a context.
    ii) the same item in another personalised sentence of their own choosing.

19.6 Role play changes

Focus	Maximising speaking practice
Level	Elementary – Advanced

Procedure

1   Start with any completed short role play, from a previous or the same lesson. For example, a short telephone call or typical social English situation.
2   Ask the students to repeat the same role play, but with one or more of the following changes:
   a) change partners
   b) change roles
   c) change a small but important detail that will then affect the outcome
   d) pretend one of the participants:
       – is feeling tired/happy/sick/angry/bored/excited/has a headache.
       – is busy and wants to finish the conversation and go.

Index

Index